"Ever wish you could fly? Me too! Yet no matter how fast I flap, truth is, I flop. Next best thing to catching a wind shear is airlifting our hearts with Courtney Ellis's offering *Looking Up*. Two things we know: in this life we will all suffer loss, and we will all long for hope. Courtney shares her flight plan from her own aerial story to her crash into grief and her recovery via the wings of hope. Need a new song? Lean in with me to Courtney's *Looking Up*, and let's feel our wings grow stronger, our minds gain perspective, and our spirits begin to soar."

Patsy Clairmont, author of *You Are More Than You Know* and cohost of the *Bridges* podcast

"I was banging my head against a wall until I read this book!"
Pileated Woodpecker

"Like an oriole stitching together its magnificent nest, Courtney Ellis skillfully weaves together theology, poetry, psychology, history, and ecology to take you on a marvelous journey. Whether you are an expert birder or a total novice, you will alternately laugh out loud and hold back tears on Courtney's bird's-eye tour through the whole gamut of human emotion—love and grief, joy and fear, anxiety and wonder—until she brings you home at last to hope. An inspiring and heartwarming read!"

Keith Gregoire, physician, author, and birder

"Courtney Ellis's wise, beautiful meditation on birds is deeply human. She gently nudges us toward the human experiences that can feel like too much— grief, loss, mortality, even overwhelming awe—and helps us to keep breathing, keep watching. In *Looking Up*, Courtney is a loving and patient guide through the unexpected turns in life, filling us with hope and pointing us toward the divine."

Dorcas Cheng-Tozun, author of *Social Justice for the Sensitive Soul: How to Change the World in Quiet Ways*

"You'll want to stay up all night reading this one!"
Great Horned Owl

"In *Looking Up*, Courtney Ellis walks us into the crucible of grief, and with faith-filled wisdom and wit—and the help of countless, wondrous birds— guides us gently through. I was drawn in by Ellis's generosity and candor, and I was kept in by her gift for storytelling. Readers will find themselves nodding along knowingly, laughing out loud, and weeping, all in the course of a single chapter. In short, this book is a delight and a balm. I recommend *Looking Up* to anyone who has ever found themselves in the valley of the shadow of death—which is to say, everyone."

Emily Hunter McGowin, author of *Christmas: The Season of Life and Light* and associate professor of theology at Wheaton College

"*Looking Up* isn't just about birdwatching. It's about birds. And it's not just about birds. It's about life. And like life, it's delightful."

Karen Swallow Prior, author of *The Evangelical Imagination: How Stories, Images, and Metaphors Created a Culture in Crisis*

"This is pastoral imagination at its finest and with a sacramental flair. In the midst of sorrow and grief, Courtney Ellis has us literally looking up to the birds all around us, then looking higher still at the Creator who reveals things about himself and what it means to be his people through these winged creatures. Her storytelling is so captivating that it has the effect of a skilled and gracious host who invites you in, makes you laugh, then cry, and then confess the deepest longings and fears in your soul. This is God's world, and God is alive and at work within it, even in our pain."

Glenn Packiam, lead pastor of Rockharbor Church and author of *The Resilient Pastor*

"Even more beautiful (if you can believe it!) than the half-eaten cheeseburger I found in the parking lot, and far more nourishing."

Grackle

"Courtney Ellis weaves together a multitude of life's threads. She skillfully tugs those threads at different times reminding us all of our interconnections—to each other, our values, and the natural world. While this book is richly about birds, it's also about much more—about how if we listen and lead with our hearts we can move through life's most difficult moments with grace."

Becca Rodomsky-Bish, Cornell Lab of Ornithology

"'My heart in hiding / Stirred for a bird,' Gerard Manley Hopkins wrote, and that stirring is felt on each page of Courtney Ellis's deeply felt exploration of grief. This is a beautiful and honest guide with which to watch for appearances of genuine hope in our own hiding hearts."

Paul J. Pastor, author of *Bower Lodge: Poems*

LOOKING UP

A BIRDER'S GUIDE TO HOPE THROUGH GRIEF

COURTNEY ELLIS

Foreword by KAY WARREN

An imprint of InterVarsity Press
Downers Grove, Illinois

InterVarsity Press
P.O. Box 1400 | Downers Grove, IL 60515-1426
ivpress.com | email@ivpress.com

InterVarsity Press® is the publishing division of InterVarsity Christian Fellowship/USA®. For more information, visit intervarsity.org.

All Scripture quotations, unless otherwise indicated, are taken from The Holy Bible, New International Version®, NIV®. Copyright © 1973, 1978, 1984, 2011 by Biblica, Inc.™ Used by permission of Zondervan. All rights reserved worldwide. www.zondervan.com. The "NIV" and "New International Version" are trademarks registered in the United States Patent and Trademark Office by Biblica, Inc.™

While any stories in this book are true, some names and identifying information may have been changed to protect the privacy of individuals.

Published in cooperation with The Steve Laube Agency.

The publisher cannot verify the accuracy or functionality of website URLs used in this book beyond the date of publication.

Cover design: David Fassett
Interior design: Jeanna Wiggins
Cover images: Getty Images: © retrofutur / iStock / Getty Images Plus, © mikroman6 / Moment, © THEPALMER, © Johner Images, © Andrew_Howe / E+, © THEPALMER / DigitalVision Vectors, © miko / iStock / Getty Images Plus, © Jose A. Bernat Bacete / Moment, © Johner Images / Johner Images Royalty-Free.

Raw Pixel: The Carolina Tit (Patus carolinensis) 122, The Mourning Warbler (Trichas philadelphia) 123, The Yellow-throat (Trichas marilandica), illustration from Zoology of New York (1842–1844) / James Ellsworth De Kay / New York Public Library; Eurasian eagle-owl (BUBO BUBO), Eurasian Tree Sparrow, Tree Sparrow (Passer montanus), illustrated by the von Wright brothers.

ISBN 978-1-5140-0716-7 (print) | ISBN 978-1-5140-0717-4 (digital)

Printed in the United States of America ∞

Library of Congress Cataloging-in-Publication Data
Names: Ellis, Courtney (Courtney B.), author. | Warren, Kay, 1954- writer of foreword.
Title: Looking up : a birder's guide to hope through grief / Courtney Ellis ; foreword by Kay Warren.
Description: Downers Grove, IL : IVP, [2024] | Includes bibliographical references.
Identifiers: LCCN 2023046329 (print) | LCCN 2023046330 (ebook) | ISBN 9781514007167 (paperback) | ISBN 9781514007174 (ebook)
Subjects: LCSH: Bird watchers–Religious life. | Bird watching–Religious aspects–Christianity. | Ellis, Courtney (Courtney B.) | Hope–Religious aspects–Christianity. | Grief–Religious aspects–Christianity.
Classification: LCC BV4596.B57 E45 2024 (print) | LCC BV4596.B57 (ebook) | DDC 201/.659807234–dc23/eng/20231122
LC record available at https://lccn.loc.gov/2023046329
LC ebook record available at https://lccn.loc.gov/2023046330

31 30 29 28 27 26 25 24 | 13 12 11 10 9 8 7 6 5 4 3 2 1

TO ANNA WOOFENDEN

a wren of a friend

IN MEMORY OF MY GRANDFATHERS

John Allen Snick (1932–2022)

and

George Delbert Belcher Jr. (1933–2023)

CONTENTS

FOREWORD

KAY WARREN

SOMETHING YELLOW, RED, AND BLACK moving extremely fast streaked past me and disappeared into a nearby oak tree.

"What was *that*?" I said aloud.

I was sitting in my backyard eating lunch in June of 2020. Like millions of other people, I was working from home, my whole life upended by the Covid pandemic. Instead of my customary travel for work—with its miles of walking or running through airport terminals, quick sprints for taxis or Uber rides, appointment after appointment—I was at home, hardly moving from the computer all day as I slowly became proficient at a previously unknown (to me) communication tool called Zoom. I recall feeling the angst of an unknown health future for myself, my family, my community, and my nation. My anxiety was high, dysregulated daily by the wild news of a world gone mad, political upheaval, and racial injustice, and physically aching to touch and hold my children and grandchildren, who could say hello only from their car as I stood on my porch. I was depressed and irritable and thoroughly out of sorts.

On that June day full of hazy sunlight, the flash of movement and color startled me. Had I really seen something?

The next day at lunchtime, I sat outside once more, the flash of colors forgotten. But there it was again! Only this time there were two flashes of yellow, red, and black—one went into the oak tree and the other into a nearby eucalyptus. I got up quickly from my chair and peered into the branches, seeking confirmation that I really had seen—what? Birds? But whatever it had been, it was gone.

The third day, I came to the backyard deliberately—eyes open, senses on alert, waiting for the flash of colors, hoping to *see* the mysterious creatures, certain they could only be birds.

They came.

Two gorgeous birds perched on a branch close enough for me to take in the pattern of their color and size; they even sang a bit of their song for me. And then they were gone—I had gotten too close.

A smile the size of Texas settled onto my face.

My heart started to pound with excitement.

I ran inside, grabbed my computer, and searched for "yellow, red, and black birds found in Orange County, California, in June."

In seconds I had my answer: Western Tanagers, "common in summer from Alaska to Baja, California."

Common in summer? How was that possible? I had lived in the same house for more than twenty-five years and I had never seen a Western Tanager. Where had they been?

Then I had my own flash. They had been there, coming every summer for who knows how many decades; I was the one who had not been there. I was at work. I was traveling. I was busy. I was blind and deaf to the magnificence of the Western Tanagers that visited annually, just I was blind and deaf to the Hooded Orioles, Black-headed Grosbeaks, White-crowned Sparrows, Lesser Gold-finches, House Finches, Red-shouldered Hawks, Northern Flickers, Anna's and Allen's Hummingbirds, Spotted Towhees, Bewick's Wrens, California Scrub Jays, American Crows, Red-winged

Blackbirds, Mourning Doves, Common Poorwills, Oak Titmice, Nuttall's Woodpeckers, White-breasted Nuthatches, Great Horned Owls, and so many other *common* birds in the canyon where I live.

I was captivated.

I sat outside every day. Morning and night. On hard days when my whole body was angsty about the chaos all around me, I spent hours in a cheap chair I found forgotten in a corner of my yard.

I read everything on the internet I could find about Western Tanagers. My curiosity became insatiable. I wanted to know about all the birds my newly opened eyes saw in my backyard—the tiny birds with the crisscross pattern on their backs, the ones with red heads and breasts that sang such beautiful songs, the iridescent green hummingbirds that buzzed by my head like tiny airplanes on a bombing run. I started ordering bird books. Bird-identification charts. Bird jigsaw puzzles. Bird feeders. First one, then two, then three, then multiple hummingbird feeders. Then a birdbath. Then plants that encouraged hummingbirds to visit my yard. Birdseed by the giant bag, binoculars, birding apps, bird organization memberships. I found the local birding store and became a known customer.

What I noticed first about the changes in me—besides the almost ridiculous focus on *birds*—was what happened to my anxiety level.

Being with the birds in my yard had a remarkable effect on my inner agitation. Because I had to be calm to enter their space and entice them to visit the feeders, my movements slowed down, my voice silenced, my approach became gentle and light. Sitting almost motionless waiting for them to decide I wasn't a threat forced my breathing to slow down as well, and after a few minutes my heartbeat slowed, my breathing evened out, and my body was at peace.

In the quiet of the corner of my yard, I could hear God's voice better. I told him I was frightened. He told me he was with me. I told him I was angry at injustice. He told me he was too. I told him I thought the world might end. He told me he was still in control of history. I told him I was sorry I had been too busy for decades to receive the gift of beauty and peace that lay five feet from my backdoor. He told me it was all right; he had been patiently waiting for me and was eager to share his creations with me. I told him I loved him and was placing my hope in him. He told me I could trust him. I told him I was forever grateful for the splendor of the birds and how much pleasure they gave me. He told me they gave him pleasure, too. I told him I would meet him there every day for as long as I was able. He told me he and the birds would be there.

What started as a quick flash of movement and color morphed into a daily practice of being with God through his birds. Just writing those words brings tears to my eyes. Their physical beauty, silly antics (have you ever seen crows chasing hawks in a celestial game of tag?), territorial disputes, squawks, chatter, songs, trills, whistles, and hoots bring me endless delight and more smiles than this Eeyore knew was possible.

It seems perfectly appropriate that Courtney Ellis and I met on a social media platform loosely associated with birds!

In the spring of 2022, a mutual friend noticed Courtney's tweets about #abirdfromthelord and tagged us both, knowing my fascination with birds. I wasn't familiar with Courtney, but when I looked her up, I discovered that she was a young pastor in a church about five miles down the road! I sent her a DM, letting her know I was thrilled there was another crazy birder nearby and invited her to get coffee sometime. She instantly replied with a big *yes!* and within days, we were sitting in her backyard, drinking tea, sharing our favorite birding books, and telling each other some of the significant stories of our lives.

Since then, we've had several tea-drinking get-togethers that included laughter, tears, joy, the ups and downs of a life in ministry, and, of course, birds. Always birds. We have shared deeply about a life in ministry—she and her husband are pastors and my husband and I served at the same church for nearly forty-three years—but as interesting as ministry is, talking with Courtney about birds makes me giddy! In delight, our voices get louder, and we use our hands to talk as we compare birding notes and recently discovered bird trivia. We frequently text each other photos of birds we just spotted, as well as make bird jokes and puns. I cheered when her dream of seeing an owl in person was realized. She whooped and hollered when I encountered my first Hooded Oriole drinking from the hummingbird feeders. Wow, do we have *fun*!

Shortly after we met, Courtney's beloved grandfather passed away, and our conversations broadened to include grief and mourning—she, her grandfather; me, my son who'd passed away several years earlier. Sharing grief with my new friend became a tender bond of affection.

This book is the equivalent of having tea with Courtney. She skillfully interweaves stories of her dearly loved grandfather with the traits and behaviors of the birds meant to teach us something about God's nearness in our times of trouble and loss. Her writing is a beautiful reflection of her: witty, articulate, passionate, elegant, and rich in spiritual wisdom and insight. Come for the birds, stay for the lovely, comforting words—or come for the lovely, comforting words, stay for the birds. Either way, you won't be disappointed.

I

LOOKING UP

BIRDING

You could do worse than to
spend your days staring at blue jays.

JULIE ZICKEFOOSE

WHEN I FIRST BEGAN BIRDING, my husband, Daryl, regarded the entire enterprise with a kind of perplexed, gentle bewilderment. In our fourteen years of marriage and preceding five years of friendship-that-blossomed-into-dating, I'd never once mentioned birds. I never really even noticed them. Then, near the end of my thirties, as sudden and unexpected as a flash of lightning on a cloudless night, the birding began. I imagine this could be annoying.

We'd be in the middle of a conversation, laying out ministry strategy or parenting logistics, sitting together with our coffee in the backyard, and I'd look up and gasp.

"What?"

"Oh my gosh, Daryl, it's a kinglet. Ruby-crowned, I think. Just . . . hold that thought. I'm going to get my field guide."

He bore with the hiking and the bird-identification apps, the growing stack of birding books, and all the feeders I hung in the backyard. He bought me binoculars for Christmas and put our three kids to bed by himself night after night during the annual spring migrations with nary a complaint. Still, I suspect a small part of him thought I might be using the hobby as a convenient escape from the daily grind of domestic life. Surely a person who'd previously shown absolutely no interest in them couldn't get that into *birds*.

Then came a month of wildfires, the air near our Southern California home too choked with smoke for easy breathing, much less hikes into the hills. Our backyard birds sheltered, their songs clipped and short, their behavior agitated. My own mood darkened with the ominous orange sky that turned our neighborhood Martian, the fine ash that blanketed our cars. We plodded on together, air purifiers running on high in our bedrooms, outdoor activities canceled or moved inside. We did okay, Daryl and the kids and me, but I couldn't shake the feeling that I was less than whole.

"I see now that you need your birds," Daryl told me. "I don't understand why, but I see that you do."

I don't always understand why, either. I never needed birds before. But now I do.

Birding is a switch that flips. Amateurs and ornithologists alike can point to a particular bird that turned the light on for them. We call it a "spark bird," the bird that changes everything forever. It may not end up being a person's favorite bird, or even a very noteworthy or beautiful or rare one, but it is a watershed. There is a before and an after, and nothing is the same ever again.

"You have a phoebe!" my friend Michelle gestured to our backyard string lights, where a small black-and-white songbird perched, flicking its tail up and down. I studied the bird for a few moments, the tuft of black feathers atop its head, its bright black eyes and tiny black beak, its white front and quick, jerky movements. I didn't yet know the words for most of what I was seeing— that the tuft of feathers was a *crest*, the bird itself a type of *flycatcher*. I didn't know the importance of precision when describing a bird: the phoebe didn't have a white front, it had a white *belly*. I didn't know it was called a *black* phoebe, distinguishable in color and size from the eastern and Say's varieties.

What I did know, in those very first moments, was that this little bird had unexpectedly captivated me. For a moment the volume turned down on my shouting to-do list and clamoring young children and creaky house projects and pinging work emails, and it was just me and this bird. A moment in time. A breath. Delight.

In that moment, I looked up.

Birds are invisible to us, until they aren't. Or perhaps they aren't invisible, not exactly. They are simply a background to the rest of life, the more immediate, louder bits. Perhaps we remember the gull that stole our cookie or the swans that paddled across a lake we frequented as children. Maybe we watched pigeons from our apartment window or fed leftover lunch crumbs to sparrows on our school playground. But mostly birds were not really a *thing*.

And then, one day, out of nowhere, the spark.

Perhaps you have a spark bird of your own, a Great Egret or Black Rail or Indigo Bunting, a tall, spindly flamingo or a tiny, buzzy hummingbird. Maybe you're contemplating putting this book down because you were expecting to read about hope and grief and here I am, yammering on about birds, which is not what you signed up for. But here's the thing: illumination is inscribed on every page of creation. "Chanting aloft in the pine-tops," wrote the poet Robert Service, "The wind has a lesson to teach."[1]

In his first letter to the Thessalonians, Paul writes that "we do not grieve" like those "who have no hope" for "we believe that Jesus died and rose again."[2] These holy reminders come to us through Scripture, but that is not their only place of speech. The natural world pulses with the heartbeat of God, and birds are a unique avenue into this understanding.

Look at the birds, Jesus tells the crowds up on the mountainside, and one by one, the people look up.[3] And Jesus begins to show each soul its dignity and value and worth.

In the book of Exodus, Moses is hard at work herding his father-in-law Jethro's sheep.[4] Anyone who has worked for an in-law knows that the pressure is on to do the job well. As Moses and his sheep meander through the wilderness, Moses' eyes are tuned, on the lookout for pitfalls and predators. He's hoping to spot a lush patch of grass or two, when his attention is diverted by a strange sight.

There, over in the chaparral, is a bush aflame. Small fires are not unusual in this parched land of heat and scrub, but Moses is drawn closer by a realization: this bush is burning, yet it is not consumed. The fire does not spread, nor does it go out. It burns and burns and burns.

Take off your shoes, comes a voice, *for the ground upon which you stand is holy.*

There is a before and an after. There is a spark and a burning. In this moment, Moses is set upon a path from which he will never return, a journey that will have its end decades beyond and hundreds of miles away from this small patch of holy ground.

Rare are the moments in our lives where we can point to a before and an after. There are graduations and marriages and births, accidents and illnesses and deaths, but mostly there are long strings of ordinary days, one after the other after the other. We wake and sleep, we eat and work, we play and rest. Everything is pretty much the same, until it isn't.

After the burning bush, Moses will face months of wrangling with the great Pharaoh of Egypt. There will be a pillar of cloud and a pillar of fire and a miraculous crossing of the Red Sea. This will be followed by decades of wandering in the wilderness. A few transcendent moments will give way to forty years of slogging obedience.

Yet God will plant reminders of his presence along this arduous journey. Bread from heaven. Water from a stone. Quail to nourish the body. God will speak to Moses. God will appear to him. God will continue to guide. Even in the slog, there is hope.

Many years before Moses, God pulled Abraham from his tents in the dead of night and called him to the edge of his camp.[5]

Look up, God told Abraham. *Look at the stars.*

In the Gospels, Jesus sees the fear and anxiety of the crowds and points them heavenward, too.

Look at the birds, says Jesus. *Are not you worth more than many sparrows?*

Every year or so Daryl and the kids and I take a whale watching tour from a marina near our home. Inevitably, a tourist or two will get seasick, even in calm waters. Then the captain will tell them to keep their eyes on the horizon. It's turned into a spiritual metaphor for me: the boat will go up and down, up and down, up and down our whole life long, but if we keep our eyes up, we can catch a glimpse of salvation.

I'm not a professional birder, or even an impressive amateur one. I feel the need to mention this at the outset because I'm no ornithologist or biologist or expert in the ways of the avian world. This will not be a field guide to the birds of Southern California or an extensive exploration of ecology or even a Big Year type chronicle of the species I've encountered. At least one chapter will describe a bird I've never even seen in person. My only qualifications for the birdy parts of this book are a deep fascination with all things avian and an even deeper love. I *love* birds.

Why? Because birds are amazing. Their biodiversity alone astonishes. There are hummingbirds that can perch on a strand of hair and pigeons the size of turkeys and cassowaries that could kill an adult man with a kick. Birds come in every color imaginable: black and white, pink and blue, iridescent greens and purples, translucent silver, spotted red. There are birds that can hear sound where we only recognize silence and birds whose songs are so complex they cannot be parsed by the human ear. There are birds that thrive in temperatures that would quickly freeze or practically cook a human. There are birds that clean up the dead. Some birds can mimic human voices; others sing hundreds of unique songs. Exquisitely beautiful birds give image to the Platonic ideal of perfection, while others look doodled by toddlers. (Who thought to place the eye of a Wilson's Snipe *there*?) There are birds with twelve-foot wingspans and at least one species without wings at all. (To be fair, that one has been extinct for over five hundred years. Poor Moa.) While the world's loudest bird can match the decibel level of a jet engine, the quietest one flies so softly its wingbeats are imperceptible to all but our most sophisticated microphones.

Even the names of birds are a delight: Fairy Wren, Elf Owl, Diabolical Nightjar, Bananaquit, Honeycreeper, Handsome Fruit-eater, Cinnamon Teal, Predicted Antwren, Spectacled Tyrant. Their collectives get even better: it's a drumming of grouse, a kettle of hawks, a lamentation of swans, a gatling of woodpeckers. Penguins come in huddles. Ravens? Conspiracies. Swallows? A gulp, of course. If you get tired of a squabble of gulls, you may be ready for a charm of finches. If a scream of swifts isn't your thing, perhaps I could interest you in a scold of jays instead?

Beyond the etymological pleasures, much of the culture itself around birding is a joy. I love the gentle nerdiness of so many bird people, their pocket-covered pants, their silly hats, their sturdy shoes, their nicknamed binoculars. (These are "bins," for those of you who are uninitiated.) I love the intense, competitive birders and the whispering introverts. I love the casual birders and the obsessives, too. I love birding's codes of ethics and ecotourism, its whimsy and wonder, its Bird of the Year, its conferences and conventions.

Beyond all of this, and perhaps most importantly, I love that birding itself is an exercise in delight, wonder, and gratitude. It teaches me to pay attention, and attention, I think, is at the very heart of what it means to be a person. What it means to extend and receive love. The more I fall in love with birds, the more I grow to love the whole of creation, standing in awe of the one who spun it all into being.

Maybe birds aren't your jam. That's okay. You can pay loving attention to whatever it is that allures you—a soul-bending jazz lick or the frost on your ski goggles or the artful crackles in a warm sourdough boule. Maybe it's children or grandchildren or rose bushes or nuclear physics or lacrosse or knitting or choir or finding the perfect skipping stone at every beach you encounter.

This story is about birds, yes, but even more than that it is about paying attention to grief as an avenue toward hope. The birds are secondary, in a way. They are my spark, but they need not be yours. What they offer to us is a particular window into what it means to be human: that to be alive is to grieve. To keep being alive is to hope.

To do either is to follow Wendell Berry's sage advice of continuing to be joyful, though we've considered all the facts. That is the heart of looking up.

It was the poet Mary Oliver who wrote that much of the task of being human is to pay attention, be amazed, and share about it. Fascination and curiosity are spiritual practices. Early in my parenting, my mother—an amateur artist—taught me to invite my children to tell me about their artwork rather than asking them, "What is it?" or worse yet, *guessing*. Nothing deflates a child like an adult saying, "Oh, what a beautiful dog!" when, in fact, the child has drawn Santa Claus.

The Psalms are a wonderful companion for learning this type of curiosity. We want prescription and command, *do this* and *don't do that*. We want a label beneath the drawing saying, "This is Santa Claus, not a dog." But the Psalms are metaphor and mystery, emotion and image, poetry and prayer. We can't kill them and pin them to a card, like Eustace Clarence Scrubb's beetles. They live and breathe and unsettle us. This is good. God intends it.

In his poem "What I Wish You'd Heard," David Wright describes his angst as a college professor when he tells his students to choose research topics they can live with for ten weeks.

> They chose the way we all do
> the most for the least
> Plastic bottles marked SODA

What he wants is to go back in time and tell them a different story:

Choose something you would hate
That will wake you up like a root beneath your sleeping bag
when you pitched your tent at the most breathtaking spot,
not the flattest[6]

We think we need answers, clarity, ease, comfort. Yet God is so often that root beneath our sleeping bag, waking us with an ache. Inviting us to look up.

Take a moment and look out a window. If you wait for a few moments, you're likely to see a bird (unless you're reading this on an airplane). What do you notice about it? Don't tell me it's *just* a pigeon or a sparrow or a crow. Don't discount a Canada Goose. Watch it. Look at it. See it.

There. You're a birder.

You can go as far down that path as you like—nearly everyone looks dorkishly dapper in a khaki vest—but really, birding is as straightforward as breathing. People can make it competitive or joyless, as they can most anything, but at its heart, birding is simply paying attention, holding still, and opening up to the wonder of natural spaces. It's cultivating mindfulness around creation. It's being present, right where we are, with what God has placed before us. Rowan Williams describes contemplative prayer as practicing awareness, "a little bit like that of a bird watcher." He continues: "The experienced bird watcher, sitting still, poised, alert, not tense or fussy, knows that this is the kind of place where something extraordinary suddenly bursts into view."[7]

To me, birding is a spiritual practice. After all, as Williams describes, awareness is at the heart of all contemplative practice. I find that birding tethers me to vital rhythms in the tending of my soul, to prayer and the study of Scripture and the love of neighbor alongside the care of creation. It helps uncouple me from legalism and performance—I can tally the birds I see like I used to mark down the passages of Scripture I read and studied, but unlike a book I can pull down from my shelf whenever I please, each bird that enters my gaze is here for a finite length of time, unpredictable and fleeting, a transient gift of delight.

To bird is to learn how to wait in stillness. To bird is to learn how to see.

Our church has a little prayer garden behind one of our worship spaces, pebbled pavers winding their way around lavender plants and ornamental grasses and a stone cross. One year, on Good Friday, I stood there watching the sun set, taking a moment in stillness before leading evening worship and—I'll just be honest—introverting after a long week of hectic ministry. In the golden beams of twilight, I watched a Mourning Dove alight on the cross, its pink feet curled over the edge, its feathers smooth and pale. I wondered what birds witnessed Jesus in the garden on the night he was betrayed.

As I watched the dove—a symbol of peace and baptism and the power of the Holy Spirit—it suddenly hit me how little I really knew. There I was, one person among billions, standing in a California garden, dressed in a black robe and preparing to testify to wisdom from beyond the grave that had been handed down in ancient texts written in foreign tongues. I realized at that moment I had nothing of my own to offer—I could not possibly be clever enough or charismatic enough or competent enough to convince anyone of anything. Horror and then fear and then blessed relief washed over me. I was not up to the task because the task was not humanly possible. God would have to show up and teach all of us how to see.

The older I get, the more I can see the wisdom of my elders. As a teenager I already knew everything. (Most teenagers do.) The words of my parents and grandparents washed over me like water off a duck's back—constantly there, but never soaking in.

My maternal grandparents lived less than an hour away from the northern Wisconsin town in which my sisters and I were raised. Most weeks we'd see them at least once—they'd bring us chocolate-frosted cake donuts from the green-roofed bakery just off the highway and we'd eat them on stools around the breakfast table, or else we'd drive over to their little lake house for dinner, winding down their gravel road with our mouths watering in readiness for the chicken and baked potatoes Grandpa cooked on his old charcoal grill.

My grandfather strung feeders across their backyard, waging war with the gray squirrels intent on stealing the seeds he intended for his chickadees and goldfinches.

"We had an oriole yesterday," he'd tell me. "I saw three robins."

"Mmm," I'd respond, searching his shelves for Archie comics. "Cool."

My grandfather was a man of few words and fewer pleasantries. He made Calvin Coolidge look chatty. But he did love animals and would talk more about them than anything else.

I recognize now what he was saying to me in his bird reports. A kind of deeper, subtler way of speaking. A language unrecognizable until a person has suffered a great deal.

He was telling me he loved me.

This book is my way of doing the same.

2

DEATH
VULTURES

Maybe we get the endings we deserve.
Or maybe the endings we practice.

DANIEL NAYERI

O N SATURDAY, I LEARN THAT my grandfather has fallen and been taken to the emergency room by ambulance. I'm in California. He's in Wisconsin. It's three days before Holy Week—the busiest seven days in the church calendar. I'm a pastor. Our young children are on spring break; our senior pastor is out of town. Daryl—my husband and copastor—and I are already both rubbed raw with exhaustion.

But Grandpa is eighty-nine and I feel the scale beginning to tip toward eternity.

Twenty-eight Turkey Vultures roost in the tree across the road from my house, hissing and squabbling on occasion, but most often sitting silent and still until it's time for them to go to work. Then they lift, one after another, out of the shaggy branches with a scuffling of leaves and heavy wings that together sound like a sheaf of paper thrown down a staircase. They ride thermals into canyons between our home and the mountains beyond, their shiny red heads black against the glaring morning sun, flying silently as they scout out the dying and the dead.

Turkey Vultures are the least sentimental of birds. They have no syrinx—the usual avian voice box—with which to chirp or sing. Instead they grunt and wheeze, and that infrequently. They don't build nests, preferring to lay their eggs on any flat and reasonably secure surface: a cave floor, the hollow of a tree, an outcropping of rock on the side of a cliff. Ungainly and awkward on the ground, they perch up high, resting until they are ready to tumble into launch, to search the underbrush, smelling for the gasses of decomposition, and then gliding down to their task.

A group of vultures is known as a committee if it's found in a tree. On the ground, it's a wake. Fitting, perhaps, as these huge, black-robed scavengers gather to pay their final respects to a deer, a rabbit, a wayward housecat. The clever, waxy skin of their heads and feet repel the bacteria of decaying flesh; their guts can handle rot that would cripple other predators. They're the janitors of the bird world. And the priests.

I stand in solidarity with them in my own black robe, graveside in the harsh early morning or beating afternoon sun—there's rarely anything else here in Southern California—reading the liturgy we Presbyterians recite over the dead, words spoken over their bodies but intended, really, as comfort for the living. There is power simply in speaking truth, in forming words that give witness to reality.

We read from Job: *I know that my redeemer lives.*[1]

Or from John: *I am the resurrection and the life.*[2]

Or, when I am given the responsibility to choose the Scripture, because sometimes a grieving family simply can't face one more decision, I read from Revelation: *Do not be afraid, I am the First and the Last. I am the Living One. I was dead, and now look, I am alive forever and ever!*[3]

For a brief time after seminary, I trained as a hospice chaplain. It was well-intentioned but doomed from the start: I was too young and unseasoned for hospice, not yet prepared to sit for hours with the dying, to bear witness to their regret or despair or acceptance or fury. The pastorate moves through the full spectrum of human experience—funerals, yes, but also baptisms and weddings, committee meetings and kickball games and conversations over coffee. Hospice was all death all the time, and I wasn't yet ready for even one. I'd come home from work, sit on the hand-me-down sofa in our half of a tiny duplex, and weep over the injustice of death itself.

"It just isn't *right*," I'd tell Daryl, mind-blown by mortality. Still, the few months I lasted continue to prove invaluable. My very first week of training, my supervisor told me repeatedly to use the word *dead*.

"People don't expire," she said. "That's milk. They don't pass on or away like a ship on the ocean. They didn't get lost, because we won't find them. They *die*."

Death unmoors us. We do not want to speak of it and yet, when it comes to our door, euphemisms grant no comfort. We must speak of what is.

This morning one of the vultures—male or female, it's almost impossible to tell—perches on the peak of our neighbor's roof. At such close range, only ten feet or so from where I sit, I am stunned by its massive wingspan as it unfolds to the sun. Adult vultures' wings can reach seventy-two inches tip to tip, six entire feet of hollow bones and glossy feathers. From this horaltic pose, the vulture dries the dew from its wings, warms its body, and bakes off any lingering pathogens from yesterday's meal. Vultures know instinctively what it took humans centuries to discover—sunlight is a remarkable disinfectant. The vulture shifts its stance, fixing me with a glittering black eye, judging my worth as predator or meal, and then, deciding I am unworthy of fear or feast, turns its attention back to surveying the neighborhood.

There's something startling about a bird bold enough to look you in the eye, primeval as a dinosaur, wild as a lion. These twenty-eight have chosen my suburban street as their home. Out of an estimated eighteen million turkey vultures in North America, I share my space with this particular score, who live and feed and preen and sleep a stone's throw from where I do the same.

The vultures didn't always live here. Years ago, before the pandemic, beloved neighbors across the street told us with tears that they were moving away to a farm in Iowa to raise their family in wilder spaces. In the weeks before they left, our three children—Lincoln, Wilson, and Felicity—and their six mourned through play: the last fort, the last game of Monopoly, the last street-bobsled-made-from-a-wagon races. Then, just days before their van pulled away for the final time, the vultures descended.

"Twenty-eight of them!" one of their middle children, nine-year-old David, told us, binoculars in hand. We discussed whether or not the sign was an ominous one—superstition and myth and metaphor mixing with Catholic and Protestant faith.

Now, years later, I find the vultures a strange comfort. A reminder of the work I'm called to do: bearing witness. Cleaning up.

Those who go into ministry for glamour don't last long. Eugene Peterson wrote that "when it comes to doing something about what is wrong in the world, Jesus is best known for his fondness for the minute, the invisible, the quiet, the slow—yeast, salt, seeds, light. And manure."[4] Ministry is much less about fancy speeches and much more about sitting quietly with people in the ache of life. Sometimes it's just shoveling crap. Other times it is funny in ways that maybe it shouldn't be, but laughter and tears are such close cousins that either can provide a welcome release.

One summer afternoon, a church musician and I walked into the lobby of an assisted living facility prepared to hold a memorial service for a beloved parishioner. I carried a black folio filled with my usual notes—liturgy and prayers, a familiar psalm and a brief word of comfort and care. A few minutes before we were scheduled to begin, the facility's activities director led us through a test of the sound system, the musician at the piano, me with a wireless microphone clipped to my blazer. We tried out the amplification—*testing, one, two*—and gave one another the nod.

I took my place in front of the gathered faces—friends and family and neighbors from down the hall, most in their eighties and nineties, acutely aware of their own mortality—and opened my folio.

"Hear now these words from Psalm twen—"

"We can't hear you!" a voice rang out a few rows back.

I checked my microphone. The switch was on, its green light glowing. I tried again. Nothing. I looked over at Kathy; she tried a few words into her microphone at the piano. Nothing there, either. I raised an eyebrow to the activities director who was frantically plugging and unplugging cords but stopped long enough to shrug, the universal gesture for, "I don't know, man, technology stinks sometimes."

I cleared my throat. A sea of elderly people, the majority of them hard of hearing, watched me shift from foot to foot. I took a deep breath.

"HEAR NOW THESE WORDS FROM PSALM 23—"

"We can hear you!" my new friend from row three piped up again. "Keep going!"

I yelled that entire memorial service, except the hymns, which our musician belted from over at the piano in a glorious contralto. She and I avoided all eye contact, knowing that if laughter began to rise up, there'd be no stopping it. Only God's grace and the two of us pretending to study the ceiling tiles averted disaster. Never have I ever felt so much like I was in a *Saturday Night Live* sketch.

Vultures are darkly comedic birds. On the ground they lurch and hop. In trees they sit hunched, looking a little put off. They are the librarian when your book is overdue, the doctor when you won't take your medication. They're not mad; they're just disappointed. No one puts a vulture on a greeting card unless it's a joke—*Heard you were sick! Don't worry, we'll wait!* Owls are symbols of wisdom and bald eagles synonymous with patriotism. Vultures are the goofy, hooded harbingers of death.

Before he was a renowned birder, a preteen Noah Strycker dragged a rotting deer carcass to his backyard in an attempt to attract vultures. It worked, and he spent days sitting rapt under a tarp, watching them pick the animal clean in a very orderly fashion, starting with its eyes and gums. By the week's end, a stripped skeleton was all that remained.

Without vultures and other scavengers, our fields and forests would steam with the stench of rotting meat. Vultures perform an essential service, quietly cleaning up the dead. We might shiver or shudder, call them creepy or macabre, but the fact is—we need these birds.

But vultures don't make it easy for us to embrace them. They don't sing. They're too big to visit backyard feeders—and they wouldn't find anything palatable there, anyway. Their plumage is simple and unadorned. Then there are their eyes.

"When you stare into the eyeball of a turkey vulture and it blinks its third eyelid . . . that is just unsettling," Strycker told Ira Glass. "They are strange, strange animals. They just have this weird, very reptilian vibe."[5]

This third eyelid is present in nearly all birds—and some reptiles and mammals as well—but it's more visible in larger species due to their bigger eye size. Called a nictitating membrane, it helps shield and moisten the eyeball. Raptors and scavengers also use it to protect their eyes from scratches and injuries when capturing or devouring prey. Seen up close, it's almost alien. We expect animals to blink as we do—the upper eyelid coming down like a window blind. But nictitating membranes often blink upward, a milky screen pulled from bottom to top like a magician's curtain.

Nature regularly blurs the lines between beauty and mystery and comedy and horror. The end of life can do the same.

"We just wanted to say," the younger daughter whispered, squeezing my forearm, earnestly staring at me through a haze of tears and mascara, "that we would really prefer there be no clowns at mom's funeral."[6]

I nodded, slowly digesting the non sequitur. The three of us—the deceased woman's two professionally dressed, middle-aged daughters and me, her brand-new, twenty-eight-year-old pastor—had left her deathbed only moments earlier. As we stood in the hospital corridor sharing a box of scratchy tissues, my mind filled with images of colorful, costumed bodies tumbling out of tiny cars.

"Absolutely no clowns," the older daughter reiterated.

"I understand," I said, nodding somberly.

Clergy remember their first funeral. In times of grief we all long for order, for a gravitas appropriately honoring the depth of our loss. It isn't acceptable to flounder, no matter how green the clergy might be. In other words, it might be a pastor's very first funeral, but it better not look like it.

Three months into my first pastorate, a little white clapboard church in Middle America's soybean country, my heart shot through with adrenaline when a beloved matriarch succumbed after a long battle with cancer.

"She took her last breath just a moment ago," her niece told me over the phone. "The whole family is at the hospital. Will you come?"

I left our church's Lenten evening service in the hands of a few willing volunteers and hopped into my aging Toyota, driving through slush and snow, thankful I was already wearing somber colors and sensible shoes.

The hospital corridor, dim in the evening light, overflowed with children and stepchildren in their forties and fifties, some in tears, others tending grandchildren or making calls. The niece who'd phoned ushered me into the room.

"Pastor's here," she said. Those gathered turned as one, quickly falling silent.

I stepped to the head of the bed and laid a hand on the woman's cooling forehead. *Always touch the dead,* the hospice chaplain had taught me. *It lets the family know you aren't afraid, that God is present here with them, even in death.*

Death didn't frighten me. What did was the specter of botching my first funeral. Determined to do God and this dear family a proper service, I led those who'd gathered around the bedside through the Lord's Prayer. Half of the family stumbled over "debts and debtors," and it was then I remembered the woman's new husband—the man she married after being widowed a handful of years earlier—worshiped with the Methodists down the street.

As the nurse arrived to prepare the body, the rest of us regrouped in the hallway. It was then that the daughters pulled me aside to impress upon me the importance of banning clowns. I considered this new information as the coroner arrived. With the family's permission, I accompanied the deceased woman to the elevator. *People often have trouble leaving their loved one,* the same chaplain had told me. *If you walk beside the body on its way to the hearse, your presence can provide a lot of comfort.*

At the end of the hallway, waiting for the elevator, the woman's husband stopped me for a hug.

"We will need to talk about the funeral," he said, leaning in so close I could hear the high-pitched whistle of his hearing aid. "It would be great if it could feature some clowning. It can be very dignified, you know."

"I think I'm being hazed," I told Daryl later that night.

"Was anyone laughing?" he asked.

"No. That's what worries me."

The next days brought a flurry of preparations—flowers and bulletins, calls to the funeral director and the organist and the volunteers who would arrange the luncheon in the church basement after the service. I met with a dozen or so members of the woman's family, all of them soft-spoken, lifelong Midwesterners, each of them firmly choosing a side on whether or not the memorial service should involve circus performers.

The woman's first husband had been a solemn and reserved farmer, working the land, the back of his neck creased and ruddy from years of driving a tractor through sunbaked fields. During her second marriage to the Methodist, she took up clowning, and her children patiently put up with their mother's new hobby. It made her happy, and her new husband was a gentle and warmhearted man who seemed unaware of the stigma surrounding creepy clowns. But after her death, the rest of her family wanted to remember her as they knew her best—before all the face paint and cheap wigs.

I can't say I blamed them. I don't plan to die anytime soon, but I've already told Daryl that if he uses one of those schlocky funeral home poems at my memorial service, I'll haunt him for the rest of his life.

"I don't even believe in that sort of thing," I told him. "But I will find a way."

Caught in the middle, visions of my first funeral turning into *Pennywise Goes to Church,* I sought a compromise: we would set up a display in the side room of the sanctuary to feature her clowning, along with her other passions—photos of her family, her quilts, her paintings. The daughters nodded vigorously. The husband sighed.

The day before the service, a handful of the couple's clowning friends dropped by my office. They didn't show up in costume, but I could tell they were the clowns, each ill at ease in street clothes without the mask of makeup. That and one of them introduced himself to me as "Bobo."

As we shuffled around the topics of death and grief, I expressed condolences along with words I never thought I'd need to say aloud in church: "No red noses at the funeral, please," I said. "No floppy hats. Definitely no seltzer water in those spray bottle thingies." The incognito clowns hung their heads. One drew a sad mouth over his own frown in the air with his fingers.

The day of the funeral arrived, dreary in the way Wisconsin becomes when it's worn itself out with gray winter days but isn't sure what to do next. I wore my new clerical collar. The daughters read eulogies. The husband's hands trembled as he held the hymnbook, tears running down his cheeks. The clowns sat together near the back and behaved themselves—not a squirt bottle in sight.

"Thank you," her husband said afterward, pulling me in for a hug.

"Thank you," her younger daughter said. "She would have loved that."

I went home both relieved and uncertain. *Would* she have loved it?

A month went by before I learned that her husband had held a second funeral service for her at the Methodist church a few days after ours. That one featured clowns. I heard it was very dignified.

We are all grieving. Every last one of us. Many griefs are temporary or small—the ice cream cone that topples to the ground, the library book we hoped to check out that's missing from the shelves, the party we weren't invited to attend. A sigh, a roll of the eyes, perhaps a tear, and we're on our way once again. Other griefs unmoor us forever—the death of a best friend or a spouse, the unthinkable death of a child. The grief of disillusionment, divorce, feeling unsafe or unseen at home. The grief of never knowing our father or mother or of living as a refugee.

Each of us carries myriad unseen griefs within us. We are a people of grief, marked by aches and wounds and loss and tragedy. Yet we exist within a culture that does not grieve well, one that experiences a great poverty of ritual and communal practice. We struggle to mourn collectively. We struggle to mourn individually. We are not typically tender to those fresh with grief or carrying the heaviness of complicated sorrow or even just taking a moment to sigh over the dropped ice cream cone, its cold sweetness pooling into the grass, its flavor so anticipated, so desired that we could almost already taste it soaking over our tongue.

I think often of a man in my childhood hometown whose wife yielded to a rapid, devouring cancer in midlife. He spent the next decade walking the streets as a shell, a ghost. He replaced the license plates on his car with new ones that read, simply, *FATE IS.*

When I am called to the bedside of an ailing congregant, sometimes I don't arrive before they die. People go out on their own terms at the end, often much more quickly or slowly than their doctors or spouses or nurses expect. Especially when death has been anticipated—the cancer's returned or the lungs are failing or the heart has reached the end of its strength—people still, it seems, have agency in their final days and hours. They let go and accept death's journey quickly while alone in their room, wanting to spare their spouse the anguish of watching the final moments. Or they hold on, waiting for spring, for an anniversary, for an estranged daughter or son to come and say goodbye. Daryl and I witnessed a beloved mentor stave off death against all medical odds until the Cubs won the World Series. People are themselves until the very end.

Grief shapes us. How we respond to grief shapes us, too. We may share it or stuff it down, navigate it or listen to it or welcome it or run from it, but none of us will escape its effects. Grief is like water in a cup, filled up to the brim—if we set that cup gently on a shelf, little by little the water will evaporate. There may be days we can take a sip or two and discover it isn't all bitterness. Or we can pretend the cup is empty, pick it up carelessly, and watch it slosh all over everything while telling ourselves we aren't all wet.

A few months into the pandemic, Daryl found me standing at the end of our driveway, tearing through the newspaper, a tornado of black and white pages sputtering across the sidewalk.

"There is no *crossword*," I hissed, grabbing at the strewn mess, crumpling it into a giant ball and storming over to the recycling bin. "I *needed* the crossword."

When I saw him stop midway down the front walk, kindness and concern etched in his face, my anger turned to hot tears that I dashed away with the back of my hand. I moved immediately to apology. How unseemly for one of the neighborhood pastors to be throwing newspapers around in her bathrobe on a Sunday morning! I told Daryl I didn't know what had gotten into me, that maybe I needed a little more sleep or to go for a walk because it wasn't like anything was actually *wrong*. We were living a white-collar quarantine. We were safe. Supplied. Healthy, for now.

I see now that I was grieving. We all were.

We all are.

Dying opens up what mystics sometimes refer to as the thin places, narrow bands between heaven and earth where the barriers between the two realms become gauzy-fine, translucent. Near the end of life, people often hear and see things that no one else in the room does. They speak with invisible loved ones who died decades earlier, or they hear music when there is none, or they see animals in the room that we cannot see.

"Do you find them comforting?" a chaplain friend asked a dying woman who kept pointing out that there were chickens roosting on her hospital bed.

"Oh yes," said the woman, who spent her girlhood on a farm. "I've missed the chickens so."

People tend to die as they lived—petulant or magnanimous or peaceful or silly or stern. Some fight until the very last moment. Others order every detail far in advance. People go quietly, loudly, with acceptance, with anger. Occasionally they die midsentence, leaving their loved ones to play a frustrating game of Mad Libs until the eschaton. Sometimes people ask for unexpected things.

At one hospital, an elderly woman had been lying prone for days when she suddenly sat bolt upright in bed, looked her daughter in the eye, and demanded, "I want an iced tea, and *not* Snapple!"

"What did you do?" I asked.

"Well, we got her an iced tea!" she said. The woman drank her tea, smiled, then lay down and died.

The vultures have lifted off and gone to their canyons. They won't be back until nightfall, when they'll wheel in alone or in pairs, land heavily in the tree, and settle their big bodies for the night. After dark, their core temperatures will fall until they approach what would be hypothermic for a human, a hibernation-like state called torpor used to conserve energy until sunrise. With very few natural predators, they risk bedding down completely in a way few other animals can. Their bodies cool like those of the dead.

Yesterday our neighbor's father died. He weathered a long, excruciating illness and held on until he could meet his great-granddaughter.

Last week they took pictures together with the new baby, laughed, wept. A few days later, he breathed his last.

What must it be like to hold on long enough for one more thing—for the Cubs, for iced tea, for a great-granddaughter to close an impossibly tiny fist around a gnarled finger just before that finger turns to dust?

I sip my coffee at our kitchen table as I look over the children's schedules. My soul is windswept, ill at ease. Next week is Holy Week, but that isn't what has me unsettled. My grandfather lies in an emergency room in Wisconsin. Here in California, in the tree across the street, I spot a hunched black back.

One lone vulture remains.

3

UNCERTAINTY

MOCKINGBIRDS

The only thing that makes life possible is permanent, intolerable uncertainty.

Ursula Le Guin

Mᴙ PHONE LIGHTS UP WITH a text. It's my parents: *The doctor says Grandpa only has two months to live.* I slip it into my pocket and head out on a walk, straining the few details I have from oceans of unknowing, struggling to listen to the quiet voice of God in the cacophony of my own soul.

Today is the day before Palm Sunday. The next eight days will include exactly six services at our church and approximately ten thousand details. It's basically final exams week, but we aren't twenty years old anymore, so the all-nighters hurt like fire and we can't get by on takeout burritos and Mountain Dew and expect to live. The kids are already asking why we aren't traveling for spring break when such-and-such friend went to Maui and such-and-such other friend went to Mexico, and we say, ha-ha, but *you* get to go to Netflix! They are not amused.

There's no way I can leave Daryl in the midst of all that needs to be done. But then the voice, not of God but of a beloved literature professor, floats through my mind.

"There's work and there's life," she told me many years ago, after mentioning she was going on sabbatical to help care for her grandkids. "This is life."

Between my time as a chaplain and my twelve years—and counting—as an ordained minister, I've held the hands of dozens upon dozens of dying men and women. There is no precise way to predict the pace at which a person's life reaches its end. A diagnosis of two months can turn into three years of thriving. People get kicked out of hospice for being too healthy. Hopeless cases revive.

But I've also witnessed people die so quickly and unexpectedly that their spouse was still in the hospital lobby, waiting for the elevator. Death can be capricious. It can come without any warning—an accident, a sudden turn for the worse, a phone call in the night. Or it can come after a series of peaks and valleys, wrenching loved ones from hope to despair and back again in a long, slow grind. There is often no way to tell.

I wish there was a method to ascertain how much time my grandfather has left, whether I should drop everything and fly back to the Midwest right now, or wait until the other side of Easter, or simply see him in three months during the summer visit with the kids that we've already booked. I'm surprised at the magnetic pull of kinship in receiving this new, difficult news. But then, Grandpa and I have always had a special bond. He's an introvert's introvert, a lover of fishing and birdwatching and silence. He decided he approved of Daryl when, in the very first year of our marriage,

Daryl drove him the six hours home from Chicago without ever asking to turn on the radio.

If I leave for Wisconsin, Daryl will parent our children alone during the busiest week of the church year. They're amazing kids, empathetic and kind and sweet and silly, but they're also just nine and six and three years old with needs that can overwhelm the two of us on a normal week. I have no doubt he'd take it on if I asked, but what if I rushed back to my hometown tomorrow when a visit next week would have been just fine? Two months is a long time.

If it is two months.

I don't know what to do.

When faced with uncertainty, we often engage in fear responses: fight or flight, fawn or freeze. I'm a freezer, shutting down until I've had time to weigh all the options, to chart a course, to make a plan. Birds tend to respond to uncertainty with flight—it's in their nature, after all. Wingéd creatures gotta wing. But not mockingbirds.

Mockingbirds are fighters, willing to take on birds much larger than themselves to protect their young or themselves or just to cause a ruckus. They're the wild partiers of the bird world. The unhinged neighbors. Mockingbirds are the second cousins who show up at every family event with a story that shouldn't be shared in the presence of children. (Ghosts! Sexcapades! A *wonderful new business proposition!*) They do not care who they bother, drown out, or inconvenience. You never know what's going to come out of their mouths, except that it will probably be a lot.

Mockingbirds mimic hundreds of other birds' songs, often at top volume, and occasionally even through the night—especially the single males, who love a full moon. There's one sitting on the peak of a neighbor's roof as I type this, a different home than the one favored by the vultures, and every time our humble house finches begin piping up to sing, the mockingbird starts his piercing repertoire anew. Today it's a mixtape of Mountain Chickadee, House Sparrow, crow, gull, Lesser Goldfinch, and ambulance siren. He's cycling through it for the fifth time. The finches seem non-plussed, but as I said, he doesn't care. It's mating season and he's showing off his equivalent of a sports car.

Our Northern Mockingbird—*Mimus polyglottos*, the only variety in North America—flips and flashes his white wing patches, a be-havior ornithologists can't find any real reason for except that it keeps with the general mockingbird persona of being very *extra*. In the four-letter birding codes used by ornithologists for research purposes like banding and bird surveys, Northern Mockingbirds are known as NOMO. Though these codes can seem almost whimsical—the Lincoln's sparrow is a LISP, the purple martin a PUMA, the tufted titmouse a TUTI—they most commonly just come from the first letters of each word in the bird's name. Still, NOMO fits the mockingbird in more than one way—it is also the exasperated cry of birders themselves when they're trying to hear a quieter bird anywhere near a vocalizing mockingbird. *Please! No mo'!*

Often when I hear birdsong in the early morning I will fling open our bedroom curtains, expecting to see dozens of feathered messengers, only to discover that it's just our resident wild-eyed, black-beaked guy, yelling at full volume in his borrowed dialects. Mockingbirds have no decorum. They can't read the room. They do what they want.

In a way, I envy them.

Unlike the mockingbird, I don't tolerate uncertainty very well. Most of us don't. God knows all, sees all, holds all, but we glimpse only these little, often nonsensical-seeming snippets of horror and glory. We posit and predict, plan and perseverate, yet this very day a drunk driver might veer into our lane or a single pancreatic cell turn cancerous or a president make an announcement or a fault line open up, and everything we thought we could count on may evaporate in an instant.

Despite living in Southern California these past eight years, I have yet to experience a major earthquake. Friends who remember the 1989 Bay Area quake or the 1994 one in Northridge have told me how unsettling it was to feel the ground beneath them—so solid, so dependable—start to rock. If our very foundation is shuddering, what then?

Yet uncertainty is simply our lot in life. We know *in part*, writes the apostle Paul. We prophesy *in part*. Even our discerning of the future is filled with holes. A really good meteorologist is still wrong 20 percent of the time.[1] We long for the fullness of knowing and being fully known, but today we stumble around, doing our best with limited information, limited understanding, limited capacity.

Unpredictability is written into the cosmos. Quantum mechanics involves an actual uncertainty principle concerning particles that basically boils down to this: we can never know all the things, and the more we know about one thing, the more uncertain the other thing becomes. Perhaps you can nail down a particle's momentum, but that means you've now lost any grasp of its position. And it isn't just the higher sciences that reach their limits: we still don't know how birds coordinate their flights in flocks or basically anything about the mating habits of blue whales or why most human beings are naturally right-handed. Dig around in any scientific field and you'll find wisdom and facts, but also wondrous mystery when the experts reach the limits of what they've yet discovered. William Dement, a Stanford scientist known as the father of sleep medicine, concluded after fifty years of study that the only real reason we need sleep is because we get sleepy.[2] The flashy dance of the mockingbird remains mysterious. Both the universe and the God who made it seem intent upon keeping us humble.

Yet we will do almost anything to eliminate uncertainty, with the exception of not wanting our television shows spoiled. And if we can't know everything right now, we like to at least assume it is possible. When Harvard University was founded in 1692, its motto was *Veritas Christo et Ecclesiae*, or "Truth for the Church and Christ." By the mid-1800s, its logo was a crimson shield featuring three books—two face-up, their pages open to illustrate the wealth of human knowledge, and one face-down, symbolizing the limits of reason and the need for God.[3] When the school was secularized, transitioning from a training ground for ministers to today's liberal arts institution, the shield was redesigned. All three books are now face-up, and the shield features a single word: *Veritas*. The journey from humility to hubris is rarely a lengthy one.

While pride will trip us up, acceptance of uncertainty can make us more resilient. People who have a greater tolerance for uncertainty are more likely to report higher life satisfaction, self-esteem, creativity, adaptability, adaptive readiness, and stamina for ambiguity. They have lower negative affect (i.e., grouchiness) and are more willing to engage in pro-social risk-taking behaviors.[4] In short, it's healthy for us to live with open hands rather than closed, controlling fists.

I have always had a low tolerance for uncertainty. My parents still tell the story of dropping three-year-old me off at Rocking Horse Preschool on a day when the class had a surprise substitute teacher. The last thing they saw as they drove away was the teacher slowly peeling my clinging fingers off the doorjamb. Though I want to believe I have changed for the better in the decades since this meltdown, I'm not sure that I have. I want to make plans and have them work seamlessly. I'd give anything to know what will happen next. Curve balls, big or small, are *so* not my jam. For example, when our car starts making a funny noise, my internal response is usually something to the effect of, "Great God in heaven, this mild inconvenience might actually end me."

Our cars are older than most professional figure skaters, so we're on a first-name basis with the mechanics at our local repair shop. I regularly marvel at the genial implacability of the seasoned guys—they're all guys—when one harried customer after the other slaps their keys on the counter and impresses upon them how *soon* this work needs to be *done.*

"We'll see what the problem is," they say. "We'll call you with an update when we know how long it will take."

These are the same people who hung a sign on their office window during Covid that said, "Mask up. Bunch of old guys work here." In the waiting room I watch a man in a suit practically levitate with impatience, typing furiously into his phone. In the corner is a woman with a cough worrying a tissue to shreds in her hands, while another sits stoically, staring at the wall. Next to me a young father entertains his daughter by rolling a tiny rubber ball toward the door and letting her retrieve it. They repeat the game again and again and again. We are all here waiting. We don't know for how long. We can fret or we can take a page from the book of the mockingbird like this father and daughter. They are facing this uncertainty by varying and adapting their own songs. They are faring far better than most in this waiting room.

If only it were easy.

When the pandemic shut everything down in March of 2020, Daryl and I tucked our children in their beds one evening and sat together numbly on the sofa.

"What are we going to do about worship?" I asked.

"It'll have to go digital," he said. "And I think we should be prepared for this to last a long, long time."

"How long?" I whispered.

"Maybe as long as two months," he said. I gasped. We were such dear, naive souls.

And here we are, years out, still mired in uncertainty. The Covid pandemic has receded, but there will likely be others. There are wars and rumors of wars; there is fear and violence and an intractable political morass. We've learned a lot and innovated a lot and discovered a lot and also, things are still so very, very uncertain.

Uncertainty can feel like an open, bleeding wound. Family members of servicemen and women missing in action often report that it would almost come as a relief to find definitive evidence that their loved one had perished. Not knowing can be the most painful of all. How can we move on without closure? How can we plan without clarity? What are we to do when the future is shrouded in mist?

Yet when I think back to those tears Daryl and I shared on the sofa on those first pandemic days, I see the kindness of God in that obscured future. Had we known we'd be navigating a crisis for dozens of months, that we'd miss birthday parties and family reunions and in-person corporate worship, that beloved members of our church would die alone, that we'd end up homeschooling for an entire academic year—something I, personally, am so not built to do—or that I would not hug my grandparents for multiple trips around the sun, we couldn't have absorbed it. We could scarcely make sense of the possibility that we'd be facing two months of upheaval.

Uncertainty is painful. But sometimes it is also merciful.

Our oldest child is just beginning to enter the world of complexity and nuance. He now senses a disturbance in the force when Daryl and I are upset over something we haven't shared with him. If it's work related, it's rarely appropriate to tell him any details, which is very difficult for him to accept. The confidentiality required of our vocations is a hard pill for an insatiably curious nine-year-old to swallow. Other times there are facts we simply choose not to let him in on yet because, as far as it depends on us, we want to slow down how hard and fast life's burdens will fall on each of our children.

One of my literature professors told his class that one day, if we became parents, we should purchase hamsters for our kids, because it's far easier to first explain what happened to an aged hamster than it is to talk about Grandma's end. Baby steps. We don't have a hamster—Daryl sees pets as a Grand Inconvenience™—but I respect the point. Progressive revelation is a necessary thing with children, letting them in on the pain of the world at the rate they can best absorb. There will be time enough to talk about Nazis and Rwanda and Pol Pot. For now, Noah's Ark can just be the story painted on the nursery room wall because pairs of animals are cute. We will get to the destruction of the flood in due course. (Not to mention Noah's later encounter with too much booze . . .) The realities of evil will find us all eventually—no need to rush. Even as adults, steeped in the pain and horror of life writ large, the particularity of tragedy will shock us awake again and again.

We wake to news that a gunman shot up an elementary school in Texas, a fourth-grade classroom at Robb Elementary School in Uvalde. Each detail emerging is more horrifying than the last—children so pulverized they are identifiable only by their DNA, survivors unable to speak after having witnessed their classmates blown to pieces, two teachers sacrificing their lives while trying to

protect their ten-year-old students, fifteen dead—no, eighteen—
no, twenty-one.

Just last Sunday I preached on Revelation 22—the tree growing
in the city of God, with leaves for the healing of the nations. I told
the story of Dr. John Cheng, a family physician serving many of
our congregants. Only a few days prior, Dr. Cheng gave his life
rushing a gunman who drove from Las Vegas to shoot down elderly
Taiwanese worshipers in a Laguna Woods church barely five miles
from ours. My voice broke as I looked into the eyes of those in our
pews, many the same ages as those who were murdered. After the
service, one of our seniors, a retired military man, put his arms
around my neck, leaned in, and wept.

It's nearly time for dinner, so I add salt to the rice and whisk
together peanut butter and soy sauce and lime juice, garlic and
ginger and pepper, and I watch my children through the window
as they squabble and play on the backyard swing. I think of the
children of Uvalde and of Dr. Cheng as I sauté onions and sau-
sages. I pour water. I slice cucumbers as my heart tattoos a lament
inside my chest. I think of one of the men of Irvine Taiwanese
Presbyterian Church, Shoei Su, who acted heroically in the
moment and later told the press, "At the time, we were not afraid.
Later, when we think about it, we're afraid."[5]

Henri Nouwen once wrote that "much of praying is grieving."[6]
Often my prayers and grief are indistinguishable. The ache in my
chest is an offering to the God who created us for peace and, in its
absence, to work for it within our homes and churches and communities. Jesus wept over Jerusalem, longing to bring healing and
wholeness to a people not yet ready to receive it. We are so very
violent. We are so very afraid.

Pastoring bows me low many weeks with just the normal trag-
edies of congregational life—the college said no, the divorce is

final, the cancer is back—but it has also taught me that stopping to perseverate will drain the energy I require to do the next thing God asks. So I stir our dinner in the skillet and breathe my grieving prayers in and out. I think of a character who reaches his end in Samuel Beckett's novel *The Unnamable.*

"I can't go on," he says. "I'll go on."[7]

At dinnertime, our three-year-old gets a splinter in her foot. We're eating outdoors at the picnic table, which is worn to roughness by the sprinklers and the sun. We need to replace it, or at least sand it down.

I duck under the table to inspect her foot and there, nestled in the grass by a table leg, is the severed head of a mockingbird, its feathers matted with blood, its eyes partially eaten by maggots.

"Oh my," I say, and Daryl peers under the table.

"Is that a dead bird?" he asks.

"Part of one."

Bereft at the delay in care, Felicity erupts into tears of anger, howling her pain and the frustration that dessert will now be delayed by tweezers and hydrogen peroxide. I scoop her up and dry her tears with my thumb, carrying her inside. We nestle on the bedroom floor so I can remove the splinter—thanking Jesus that it isn't deep enough to require anything but a gentle pluck from outside her soft, pink skin. I fill up the bathtub and set her gently in the warm water.

"Are you feeling any better?" I ask. She nods. I head down the hall to the linen closet for a towel. Then I hear her sing.

"You gave me a heart," the sweet kazoo-voice of my tiny child drifts from the bathroom, interspersed with sounds of quiet splashing, "and you gave me a smile. You gave me Jesus and you made me a child." She's learning this song at preschool, and a few of its words fascinate her. She pauses to splash for a few seconds.

"A *child*," she says. "Mom, a *child*."

I begin to weep.

"Mom!" she calls. "Come here for a second! I want the strawberry soap!"

I swallow hard.

"Coming, baby girl."

After the kids are tucked in for the night, I put on rubber gloves and pick up the mockingbird's head, turning it over in my hand. Yesterday I'd stepped across a carpet of silver and black and white feathers to get to the car, and now I know why. I wonder about the new neighborhood cat, a well-groomed tabby sporting a tag that says, "Black Mamba." Mockingbirds have only a few natural predators—owls, hawks, snakes, cats. In my mind, I hear the voice of every ornithologist I've ever spoken to: *keep your cats indoors.*

"Daryl?" I ask, poking my head inside the front door. "I want to keep the bird skull." He looks up from his reading.

"I'm sorry, you *what*?"

"I'll boil it and then bleach it with peroxide. It's safe to do, with proper precautions."

"Why do you know that?"

"I was homeschooled."

"Will you use a pot we don't, you know, eat out of?"

"Of course."

He waves me in and then retreats to the back of the house, un-interested in mockingbird soup.

I clean the skull in the yard and then tidy the kitchen as it simmers on the stove. I lose myself in packing the children's lunches, a chore I usually detest that feels, on this night, somehow sacred. I make sure Felicity gets her favorite yogurt flavor; I put in extra animal crackers; I give them each an apple juice instead of their usual water. I pray for Shoei Su and the family of Dr. Cheng, for the pastor of Irvine Taiwanese Presbyterian Church just up the road. I wonder what it must be like to return to a worship space after scrubbing blood from the carpet. I pray for the parents and grandparents and siblings and survivors in Uvalde.

By the time I turn back to the stove, the bird's beak has weakened, and the skull has begun to flex, its occipital bones crumbling to nothing. I've kept it on the burner too long. I watch the steam rise as I wait for it to cool, my mason jar of peroxide and water already prepared but no longer needed. In my distraction, I've ruined this beautiful, macabre thing. I pour out the jar and then carry the skull out to the yard, pausing to breathe in the night air, stepping through feathers still strewn across the sidewalk. I think of all the lunchboxes sitting empty tonight in Uvalde, just two days before the end of the school year.

I ponder keeping the kids home in the morning, safely ensconced on our property where the greatest threat to them is a splinter from the picnic table, but I know I have to send them to school. The next days hold parties and concerts they've anticipated for weeks—the first celebrations of their kind after years of Covid precautions. I wish there was a way to know what the future held. But if there was, could I bear it? Could any of us?

I think of how difficult even small uncertainties can be. Felicity cried all afternoon when her best friend got a tummy bug and had to miss a day of preschool. Lincoln won't watch a movie with us unless we promise him no animals die. Wilson once wept for hours after seeing an unhoused woman on the side of the road and learning she didn't have a warm bed waiting for her. Children are so tender.

We, too, are tender. We cannot handle the weight of all the truth at once, or even spread out over time. There's a reason death entered the garden after Adam and Eve ate from the tree of knowledge. Only God can know it all, hold it all, and live. Jesus himself tells us that each day has enough trouble of its own. The mist of uncertainty is its own grace.

Painful, painful grace.

Northern mockingbirds are mist-colored, foggy gray fading to white on their bellies, with long, spindly legs and bright, intelligent eyes. They aren't beautiful, not really, but they are scrappy and interesting to look at, which is, in its own way, even better. In the early 1800s, mockingbirds were often kept as pets, with the best singers prized for their voices. Thomas Jefferson owned one and allowed it to follow him around the White House, a perky little bird named Dick.[8] In typical colonizing fashion, so many mockingbirds were pilfered from their forest homes that they almost disappeared from the East Coast entirely.[9]

Pet mockingbirds became trendy, the death-knell for many birds in early American history. Though this affected their wild breeding populations, at least the pets remained alive. In the late 1800s and early 1900s, an estimated five million birds per year, including Snowy Egrets, Blue Herons, and Sandhill Cranes, were slaughtered in the United States so their feathers (and sometimes even their entire bodies) could be used to decorate women's hats. The Migratory Bird Act Treaty of 1918 put a stop to this, praise God.[10]

Feathers are beautiful. Mockingbirds are fascinating. The very qualities that draw us to notice and appreciate the beauty and wonder of birds nearly led to their extinction because we struggle to find any sort of middle ground between loving something so much we consume it or else overlooking it entirely. But each ecological choice has a cost. As Wendell Berry wrote, "Whether we and our politicians know it or not, Nature is party to all our deals and decisions, and she has more votes, a longer memory, and a sterner sense of justice than we do."[11] At its best, birdwatching is an exercise in a healthier type of loving attention—one where we notice and nurture without disrupting or destroying.

The American Birding Association asks that its members follow a code of ethics. Birders pledge not to disrupt habitats, trample vegetation, or sneak onto private property without permission. They are also invited to promote bird-friendly practices like keeping cats indoors (I'm looking at you, Black Mamba), adding treatments to windows to help prevent bird strikes, and landscaping with native plants. In my first days of birding, I was grateful for the ways the guide helped me think holistically about my impact on the natural world. Birding could be about more than just my momentary appreciation and delight—it was an opportunity to preserve, protect, and promote ecological health so that both my neighbors and my children's children's children would have the opportunity for the same joys.

I'll admit, there are times I want to bend this code of conduct. It reminds birders to "always exercise caution and restraint when photographing, recording, or otherwise approaching birds,"[12] but when there's a rare bird within my line of vision, I want to rush right in and get the best line of sight possible. I want to make the thing happen rather than wait and give space and possibly miss it. I hate the uncertainty. But therein lies one of the beautiful challenges of birding: accepting that it is all grace. Birders live in hope. We hike into deserts and jungles and tundras, enduring heat and bug bites and freezing weather. We string up feeders and learn to mimic calls to draw birds from their hiding places (when appropriate, that is—I haven't forgotten the code!). But in the end, even with all our efforts, every bird that alights in our line of vision is a gift, even the most bossy, boisterous mockingbird. Birdwatching is a school for receiving the bountiful goodness of God, for acknowledging that the Spirit blows where it will and cannot be snatched from the air and caged.

This is a hard lesson. Uncertainty can feel like chaos. When we are unsure what is going to come next, anxiety is nearly always close at hand.

"At least we had food in Egypt," the children of Israel gripe to Moses, omitting the fact that they were also slaves. Yet uncertainty is not the same as anarchy. It's simply unknowing. Those of us with faith remind one another—and must keep reminding one another—that this cliff edge is not the lip of a yawning abyss but instead the tipping point where we fall directly into the hands of God.

My husband and I met more than two decades ago as college freshmen. Daryl, already a lover of theology, often railed against authors and scholars who "punted to mystery" when they reached their limits. "Things can be *known*," he would say. "We mustn't be so *lazy*."

Today, with a PhD in systematic theology and nearly a decade in pastoral ministry, he is much quicker to say, "I don't know. Maybe. God can be mysterious."

My particular demands of God are met most often with silence, its own type of mystery. What answer might possibly satisfy me? I don't know. One of my mentors says he doesn't believe God often gives us answers but instead helps us live with the questions. In Scripture, God rarely shows up with a straightforward response to a *why*. Instead, he reframes or offers the comfort of his presence.

When Job rails at God, God responds by pointing him toward the natural world.

"Where were you when I laid its foundations?" God asks. And Job, wrecked in body, mind, and spirit, scraping sores from his body, mourning the death of his children, is silent.[13]

I don't always love this response from God. I spy spite; I call out cruelty. I keep asking why. But perhaps God might help me to live with my questions, trusting that hope is a long story. Maybe the natural world has balms to offer us in our suffering, even if it holds no cure.

A social media friend spent months leaving a benediction for her followers each night: "You are not alone, and this will not last forever."[14] On rougher evenings, when my soul feels like one big bruise because I wasn't prepared for what the day would fling at me, I find myself repeating her words aloud in my kitchen, my bedroom, my backyard. You are not alone. This will not last forever. It's an echo of the wisdom in the Book of Common Prayer and the Liturgy of the Hours and the Psalms. It's the promise given to the people of God in the exile and to us today in our own exilic seasons big and small. When we run short on words to explain, to express, to elaborate upon the myriad ways the world slowly strips off our skin, the words of other faithful believers can be a guide and balm. Perhaps that is why mockingbirds sing borrowed songs.

In *The Genius of Birds*, Jennifer Ackerman describes the oft-maligned mockingbird not as a mimic but as a cover artist. She writes, "To my ear, this Delaware bird sang Carolina wren the way Bette Midler does the Andrews Sisters. It may be true that he was a shameless sampler, strewing about phrases from titmouse, chickadee, the sweet liquid song of a wood thrush, but he tucked them into his song the way Shostakovich weaves his symphony around a simple folk melody."[15] Perhaps mockingbirds showcase

all any of us can do—sing the oldest songs in the best ways we
know how, unique to our own wandering, warbling voices and
volumes. "Follow me as I follow Christ," Paul writes, a bold proc-
lamation for anyone other than a mimic of the one true God.

I still don't know what to do about my grandfather's diagnosis. It is
a small miracle that, on the cusp of turning forty, I still have all four
grandparents living. In Oscar Wilde's *The Importance of Being Earnest*,
Lady Bracknell berates the play's newly orphaned protagonist: "To
lose one parent, Mr Worthing, may be regarded as a misfortune;
to lose both looks like carelessness."[16] My situation feels like the
inverse: that somehow I must have been particularly conscientious
to enjoy each of my grandparents into my late thirties when, of
course, I can claim no responsibility for their longevity.

I'm primed to sing the songs of Holy Week—the "Hosanna" of
Palm Sunday and the "Stay with me, remain here with me" of
Maundy Thursday and the "Were you there when they crucified my
Lord?" of Good Friday. But perhaps God is asking me to add an
unexpected chorus to a concert program I thought was already filled.

I sit on the edge of the paved walking path, its asphalt hot under
the beating sun, and pull out my phone to look for a plane ticket
home. It's hard to get there from here. There's nothing available at
this short notice that would arrive at the airport closest to my
grandparents' house. There's only a single seat left on a journey
with two connections: Orange County to Chicago to Detroit and
then on to Mosinee, Wisconsin, where I'd have to then drive an
hour and a half north. That flight is over a thousand dollars. I text
Daryl. He's out at the home improvement store with the kids,
buying edging for the garden. *My gut is that Grandpa is going to go fast,*

I tell him. *There's only one flight left that can get me there on Monday. I think I need to take it. I think I need to go home.*

Book it, Daryl responds. *We will figure out the money later.*

There can be no price tag on final goodbyes, even though later we will need to pay the price. I will leave on Monday. Great and Holy Monday. Thousands of years and thousands of miles away, Jesus would be pivoting from Palm Sunday to his week of passion. I put my phone back in my pocket and look up. A song sparrow eyes me from the edge of a thicket, quiet and waiting.

4

LIFE

SPARROWS

The world is burning, and there is no time
to put down the water buckets.
For just an hour, put down the water buckets anyway.
Take your cue from the bluebirds,
who have no faith in the future
but who build the future nevertheless.

MARGARET RENKL

I BOOK THE LAST AVAILABLE FLIGHT to rural Wisconsin at this eleventh hour, three airplanes on two different carriers with two separate connections. I'll be in transit for over twelve hours, and that's if nothing goes wrong. It is hard to get there from here. It's hard to get there from almost anywhere.

The first time I drove Daryl to my parents' house from our Chicago college, he looked at the trees speeding by our window and asked, "Why do we keep going? Isn't this as good a forest as any?" Born and raised in Los Angeles, he believes that the many inconveniences of rural Midwestern life—clouds of mosquitoes, months of subzero temperatures, no Home Depot—tend to outweigh its charms.

My first connection will be tight—a short hour in Chicago—and because I'm flying on competing airlines, I'll land at a different terminal than the one where I'll board my next plane. I am preparing for a sweaty airport run to have even half a chance to make it. I have no checked bag—just a backpack and a gym bag stuffed with gifts for my family plus my T-shirts and socks, a soft cardigan, and a gauzy, flowered scarf. When the specter of death hovers, I've learned it is a good idea to dress for warmth and softness and gentle cheer.

A few minutes after five a.m., I park at John Wayne Airport and shuffle through a lengthy security line. I haven't flown much recently, but it seems most passengers now would rather be early than late, and we move slowly together past tables and through scanners, removing shoes and laptops, tossing the occasional water bottle into a recycling bin. I arrive at my gate at 5:42 a.m., second in line to speak with an agent. To make these flights work, I'll need help.

The gate agent arrives at her standing desk already breathless and annoyed, her strawberry blonde hair feathering out in waves. She is, I fear, one of the Rule Followers™. Daryl believes that even the best rules—minus those from the Almighty, of course—are meant to be questioned, if not broken. I am and always have been a Rule Follower™ (eldest daughters are rarely anything else), but in this moment I'm hoping for an employee who errs on the side of grace. I pray to see a spark of humanity in her eyes, to be seen as a person, not just a passenger.

She glances up from her computer screen. "We are not even open yet. Wait over *there*," she says, and points to an identical spot on the carpet three feet to my left. "We will see you in a few minutes," she says, turning back to ferociously clickety-clack her keyboard.

I am clearly just a passenger. There are rules.

I dutifully move over, adopting the posture a journalist once described as the "kindly brontosaurus."[1] Nonthreatening, wide-eyed, and too benignly present to ignore. I know I won't receive any assistance if I'm aggressive. It's not my style anyway, and after all, it's 5:48 a.m. and no one is in the mood for a battering ram. Within seconds another agent, newly arrived, motions me forward.

"My grandfather is dying." The words surprise me, even as I say them. The gravity of the situation takes shape as I put voice to it. Tears spring to my eyes.

"I am so sorry to hear that, Sweetie," he says. He is young, perhaps ten or fifteen years my junior, his black hair slicked back, his glasses rectangular and striking.

"I am doing all I can to get to him in time and I have a really tight connection," I say.

He nods. He is listening.

"My seat is all the way at the back of the plane. Is there any way I could be moved closer to the front?" He looks to his screen, taps a couple keys, and proclaims my salvation.

"There's a middle seat in row fourteen." He prints off a new boarding pass and pauses to look me in the eye as he hands it over. "I really am sorry about your grandfather."

I spend my life shepherding others through grief. I am soft-spoken at the hospital bedside, calm at the memorial service, clear at the graveside committal. Though I've buried congregants who were also dear friends, mentors, second family, my tears come later; I've trained them to wait until the drive home so I can keep my focus on those who are rawest in their own fresh grief. Their pastor is not their daughter, after all, nor their mother or sister or best friend. I have a role to fill, to be the one who points to the shepherd in the valley of the shadow, not to my own grief. This is one of the unseen burdens of ministry: to grow to love people deeply, to hold their fears and secrets and confessions and hopes tenderly, and then most often to mourn them alone.

But today I am a granddaughter first. Today I have the airplane seat I need, one that gives me a fighting chance to make my connection and get home in time to tell my grandfather I love him before morphine takes away his pain and his presence. To the gate agent, I wasn't a passenger or a pastor, a ticketholder or a problem to solve. I was a person like him. It was the "Sweetie" that bowled me over. A word of tenderness in an impersonal, harried terminal at 5:49 a.m. Nothing breaks through a meticulously constructed dam of professionalism and self-control like a little bit of kindness.

I stuff my bags into a bathroom stall with me, lock the door, and crumple into tears.

It is a mark of divine love that even in our striking sameness—aortas pumping and synapses firing and five toes on each foot—we are each utterly singular. There are over eight billion humans on this planet, but you are the only one finishing this sentence at this split second, breathing unique molecules of air that have been floating on this planet for thousands of years but somehow just arrived in front of you in time to oxygenate your particular lungs. No one shares the same color pattern in their irises or had the same first kiss or will fall asleep tonight in the exact same position. In *The Weight of Glory*, C. S. Lewis writes, "There are no ordinary people. . . . Next to the Blessed Sacrament itself, your neighbor is the holiest object presented to your senses."[2] We started on this planet with the very breath of God in our lungs, formed from the dirt and invited to transcendence. "Beloved dust," Lisa Sharon Harper calls us, and that about sums it up.[3]

A decade and a half ago, Daryl and I tumbled out of an airport shuttle in Mexico, pale from a Chicago winter. We walked up to our hotel's front desk, blushing and tittering, and told the desk clerk that it was our honeymoon. The bridal magazines told me to mention this. Sometimes there would be a free upgrade, they said. Sometimes a bottle of champagne. But the receptionist just sighed.

"It's Cabo," she said. "It's everyone's honeymoon."

Jaded from hordes of tourists, she saw only sameness. But together in those first tender days of marriage, we discovered new depths to the person we'd vowed to love and cherish—depths we continue to mine to this day. And even this person, the one I know best, the one with whom I've debated theology and rocked babies and weathered flu bugs, the one I rely upon in my weaknesses and support with my strengths, the one with whom I've shared a bed and, for many years, a church office, too, remains a divine mystery to me.

It would be enough for God to create such specificity among just the human family, stamped as it is with the *imago Dei*, but the natural world is extended this same grace and goodness. Every tree and twig and leaf paints its own rare swath of color. No two ladybugs have the same precise pattern of spots. Birds sing their one-of-a-kind songs, particular not only to their species but fine-tuned to their geographical locations, like people's regional accents. Each individual bird in each individual species is unique. The Red-billed Quelea, for example, a weaver native to sub-Saharan Africa, nests in colonies of millions that have been known to stretch over twelve miles long. Within these massive congregations of fluttering, twittering birds, each parent knows exactly which near-identical chick belongs to them. Where we see nothing but a sea of feathered sameness, the birds recognize the subtle signs that mark their nestling as their own.

Much of our modern economy is fueled by uniformity. We purchase identical smartphones, washing machines with interchangeable parts, bags of candy designed as spotless clones of one another. It's notable when our fast food meal looks even slightly different than it usually does. (Who doesn't love a rogue onion ring in their curly fries?) Henry Ford learned to churn out cars at a high rate of speed and profit because every bolt and belt and gasket could fit seamlessly onto every identical automobile. Sameness is profitable. It's also rote.

But one of the marks of God's good creation is that even seemingly indistinguishable things are never exactly the same. Each wildflower is special. Every mustard seed will produce a slightly different tree. The very ground beneath our feet pulses with holy, diverse microbes.

And then there are the sparrows.

Sparrows are everywhere. They live in every corner of North America, from the southern tip of Mexico to northernmost Canada, and nearly every country on earth. There are thirty-five different types of sparrows in the United States alone, and an estimated 140 worldwide. Just hiking the trails within a five-mile radius of our home I've encountered House Sparrows, Song Sparrows, Spotted Towhees, California Towhees, Lincoln's Sparrows, White-crowned Sparrows, White-throated Sparrows, Dark-eyed Juncos, Vesper Sparrows, Chipping Sparrows, and one particularly curious Fox Sparrow. Sparrows are the wild grasses of the bird world, blending into the landscape in ways both unnoticed and ubiquitous. Christmas decorations feature turtle doves and French hens, swans and peacocks, but sparrows are all Ordinary Time. There is a *lot* of Ordinary Time.

Take just the House Sparrow, for example. Of the estimated 50 billion individual birds on earth, 1.6 billion of them are House Sparrows.[4] These Old World sparrows are a different genus from New World varieties like Savannah and Swamp Sparrows that originated in the Americas, but they share many similarities in size and diet and behavior. You probably have at least a handful of House Sparrows near where you live, whether you're reading this book in Florida or Seattle, Finland or Syria. An invasive species not native to North America, House Sparrows now live in every state in the United States, down into Mexico, and well up into Canada. They're all over Europe and the Middle East, Africa, Asia, the eastern side of Australia. They nest readily and haphazardly almost anywhere—a hedge, an eave, a tree, a garage, a broken-down car. House sparrows have been spotted two thousand feet underground in a British mine and up on the eightieth floor of the Empire State Building.[5] A small flock of them squawk at me from a neighbor's hedge when I head out on my walks. On a recent vacation, we watched a pair peck a pizza crust to bits on a Los Angeles bistro table. They flit under the chairs at my favorite donut place, cocking their heads as they hop from sweet crumb to sweet crumb. House Sparrows are omnipresent.

It can be easy to despise what is familiar. We hunger for newness and novelty. Birders will travel mile after mile for a glimpse of a rare species, but tell an avian aficionado you've seen a sparrow and they will likely shrug. We've *all* seen a sparrow, usually when we weren't even looking for one.

Even if you're really into birds, sparrows aren't that interesting at first glance. They tend to be smallish and roundish and brownish, lacking the flash of their more colorful songbird cousins. Birders call sparrows "LBJs"—little brown jobs. In Egyptian hieroglyphs, cats and crocodiles were revered and feared, while sparrows showed up only as a determinative, added to make another word mean "small, narrow, or bad."[6] Even their collective term is derogatory: a group of sparrows is known as a quarrel. They often snap up newly sown seeds and steal precious grain intended for people or livestock. In the late 1950s, China instituted a campaign against "the four pests," including rats, flies, mosquitoes, and sparrows. As people worked to decimate the sparrow population—often by banging pots and pans until the frantic birds, afraid to alight on their usual perches, fell to the ground in exhaustion and were then quickly netted or speared—the obvious thing soon happened: insect populations exploded.[7] Even pests have their places, often to keep other pests in theirs.

But it can be easy to take what is familiar for granted. We want to escape from the daily grind; we long for new experiences and perspectives.

"I can't believe I have to go through my whole life with this *same face*," a high school friend once bewailed. "I'm only seventeen and already *so tired of it*."

Yet common things are precious to God, knit into the fabric of his purposes. It's one reason God uses plain old water for baptism, and bread and wine—ever-present and easily affordable in Jesus' day—for the Lord's Supper. Jesus was baptized in the Jordan River not because it was particularly holy but because it was right there. Jesus points to wildflowers, planted by no farmer, tended by no gardener, to remind us of the Father's providence. He speaks of seeds and coins and fields and trees. Jesus talks about the weather not because he's making small talk but because the simple things that make up our days have profound stories to tell about who God is. About who we are. About how and what and whom God loves.

"Are not two sparrows sold for a penny?" Jesus asks. "Yet not one of them will fall to the ground outside your Father's care."[8]

The commonness of sparrows is part of their glory, their ordi-nariness one piece of what makes them special. Sparrows are everywhere, but even within their vast populations, a single bird is unique, with a slightly different marking pattern, personality, history, nesting spot. Even with 1.6 billion House Sparrows and 319 individual species of New World Sparrow, every one is individually crafted, much like the normal, humble days that each come to us but once.

Sparrows are also a reminder that God's care is not dependent on our own transcendence or charisma or beauty. Everyone notices a peacock, but sparrows can blend in until we stop seeing them at all.

God never does.

In the ancient days of Israel, Isaiah gave a warning. The people had turned from God and from the goodness and care and love of neighbor that God commands. Their hearts were beginning to harden. God instructed Isaiah:

> Go and tell this people:
>   "Be ever hearing, but never understanding;
>   be ever seeing, but never perceiving."[9]

It was curse and warning: *this is what you will become if you continue down the path you've chosen.* Disobedience to God's call dulls our senses and darkens our awareness. It is faithfulness that guides our steps toward wonder. We make the choice a hundred thousand times a day, and each time we choose, our path overlaps with or diverges from the divine way. Will we see or not see?

I am certain I've failed to notice thousands of sparrows over the course of my life, perhaps more. This is not a devastating moral failing, of course. It's called paying attention because it costs something. Sometimes attention must be paid to driving or working or tending children or making sure the pasta doesn't boil over. Yet part of me grieves for all the astonishment that's passed me by when I've been looking down or away or even looking up but without really seeing. Poet Mary Oliver reminds me to pay attention. Novelist Jesmyn Ward writes of being a person who burns and hopes. Each day is laid out with a buffet of delights; it is up to us to pay the attention we will, with money that cannot be set aside for tomorrow. Manna rains down in the wilderness, unable to exist anytime but here and now, wafers sweet on the tongue. The divine melody plays notes as ephemeral as the wind, each rung out for an instant before dispersing into the morning mist.

On my second flight, the one between Chicago and Detroit, I look down at the cup of ginger ale on my tray table, drumming a hand on my right thigh where, underneath my jeans, a Song Sparrow lies in black ink.

Song Sparrows are masters of music. A single Song Sparrow's repertoire can include over two hundred different tunes. Most often my local ones start what sounds like the opening notes of Beethoven's fifth symphony—*dun dun dun DUNNNNN*—but that's only a single favorite from their massive avian collection. One study found that, much like mockingbirds, male Song Sparrows develop a thirty-minute "playlist" that they will repeat or shuffle according to the preferences of nearby females.[10] They sing in the rain, in the sleet, in the hail, at the height of summer's heat. They're my favorite bird—I literally have one tattooed on my leg, and I am not what you'd call a *tattoo person*. I've noticed that I often spot Song Sparrows in moments of real sadness or desperation or need.

"All creation sings," the psalmist writes, and sometimes God puts that song right where I need to hear it.[11]

My heart is on edge wondering what I'll be walking into. I will be in town fewer than forty-eight hours—it is Holy Week, after all—and yet I suspect the compressed emotions of this trip will spill over into Maundy Thursday and Good Friday and Easter Sunday even after I've returned to California. This will almost certainly be my final goodbye to the man who smells like Heileman's Old Style and Swisher Sweets, who taught me to love the outdoors and every animal except the squirrels—he hated squirrels—and to be unafraid of silence. Grandpa loves silence.

To add to the layers of complication, I haven't been home since the pandemic began. Covid revealed a lot within every community about how our choices affect everyone else's. There is nary a family—nor a church—where this was particularly pleasant. The day before I boarded this plane, my dear friend Anna reminded me not to try to do too much on this short, emotionally intense trip.

"Pace yourself," she said. Anna is a pastor, too, and deeply wise. She understands that the stresses of Holy Week can be difficult to bear, even without a dying loved one. She's right, of course. She nearly always is, so I tap my Song Sparrow through my jeans and repeat my goals to myself: say goodbye, be gentle, care for my grandmother, and try to save enough in my reserves to lead our congregation through Holy Week upon my return. I've brought fancy chocolate as a balm and peace offering. We don't agree on everything, my family and I, but we all agree on chocolate.

Hours later, waiting to board my final plane in Detroit, a House Sparrow sails down from the rafters. I feel a pang of worry for him—how will he survive indoors? What will he eat? Then he flits over to an overflowing trashcan and shakes loose a yellow Potbelly's wrapper, liberating half a sandwich. Oh.

A few years ago I wouldn't have spent any time with this sparrow, ready instead to crack open a novel or browse an airport bookstore. But today I watch him, his strong beak, his gnarled feet, his gray breast and cinnamon cap, his attuned-but-not-fearful glances at passersby. He makes quick work of the sandwich bread, dissecting it with the precision of a picky preschooler whose potatoes touched his peas.

I've heard a variation of it from half a dozen people now: *I wasn't a birder until the pandemic. When everything shut down and I found myself at home, I started looking out the window—really looking—for the first time since I was a kid.*

This was my story, too. In March of 2020, a few days before the world shuttered, my friend Michelle pointed out a perky Black Phoebe perched on our string lights, flicking its tail and surveying the backyard grass. It came back the next day, and the next. As the president held press conferences and the NBA shut down and I waited on updates about a nearby pastor friend headed to the hospital and then sent to the ICU and then put on a ventilator, I watched the phoebe and it watched me back. A question bubbled up: *What else haven't I been noticing?*

The pandemic sparked birdwatching as a new interest for hundreds of thousands of people. In March and April of 2020, sales of birdseed and birding accessories grew by over 50 percent,[12] and downloads of the Cornell Lab of Ornithology's Merlin Bird ID app doubled.[13] In the face of sickness and death, a teetering economy and school shutdowns, churches moving to digital worship and a contentious election simmering on the horizon, thousands upon thousands of people began looking up.

I haven't been back to Wisconsin in a long time. It's hard to get there from here in more ways than one. Our lives in California have overflowed with pastoral need, vocational stress, and pandemic uncertainty, not to mention the pure physical exhaustion of parenting three young children that sometimes still leaves me gasping for rest. There are days I don't have the bandwidth to stop by the grocery store, and on those days the idea of packing for a cross-country visit is on par with building a rocket to the moon.

We are all going back later this summer, though. Daryl and the kids and I need to be together with the extended family. We want to be together with them; it's been too long. We purchased tickets months ago, eager to have the kids hug their great-grandparents and swim in the lake and get into mischief with their cousins, committed to tending relationships that have suffered from distance, differences of opinion, and divided politics. But this unplanned solo visit of mine is its own rite of passage. The past months' crucible has broken and remade and strengthened and devastated all of us.

"The election was brutal on families," a friend's therapist told her, "but that was nothing compared to Covid."

After all of the uncertainty and hard conversations, I'm still putting pieces back, finding new ones, letting go of old, learning where to draw boundaries and where to stretch and bend and bear with love. I expect I will be recovering from these strange and apocalyptic years forever. Perhaps we all will.

Then there's my grandfather's failing health and grim diagnosis. I don't know how the waves of anticipatory grief will hit each of us within the family, individually or collectively. I'm bringing with me a bundle of experience with death and dying, hospital bedsides and hospice visits and graveside committals and church funerals, but professional experience falters in the face of personal loss. It's why surgeons are ethically prohibited from operating on family members—there is no real objectivity, no possible critical distance when it's your loved one open on the table.

I once sat at an elderly congregant's bedside as he struggled through the process of active dying. People tend to turn deeply inward before their final breaths; dying is at least as hard a task as living. The man's hands and feet grew mottled and began to cool. His breathing slowed and rattled. His children were gathered, all of them in their fifties and sixties, one a longtime hospice nurse. I deferred to her expertise as she talked us through what was to come. She stroked her father's hand as he drew a particularly long, shuddering breath and then went still.

"He's gone," she said, erupting into tears and draping her arms across his chest to hold him close. Then he drew another shuddering breath. And another. She cleared her throat. Leaned back. A sibling cleared his throat. Another began to titter.

"Guess not."

We may think we know how we'll react when it is our turn to sit on the knife's-edge, the thin place between heaven and earth, sending our own prayers up in quiet desperation, but the truth is that not one of us knows for certain. I spend my life walking with others through their grief, but I do not know what it will feel like to hold this particular one so closely and to witness it mirrored in the eyes of those I love.

I'm not ready.

But the kind gate agent at John Wayne and my airport sprint have done their work. I made my connection back in Chicago. Now I'm boarding in Detroit. The House Sparrow finishes his sandwich and takes to the rafters again. I stand, shoulder my bags, and walk toward the jet bridge.

I'll know more soon enough.

5

END TIMES

OWLS

They told me the older I get
the more conservative I would get
but what happened is, the older I get
the more I think about owls.

Paul Wallace

T HE DAY I LEARNED the San Diego Zoo has a live feed of its
Burrowing Owl exhibit, I got absolutely nothing done.

"They're feeding their babies!" I called to Daryl.

"Mmm," he said.

"They're bobbing their heads!"

"Mmm," he said.

"I am going to show the kids after school today, and they will be
so much more excited about this than you are," I said.

I did. They weren't. But here's the thing: owls are amazing. The
more I study them, the more fascinated I become.

Owls are one of the few types of bird with front-facing eyes, which, combined with their downward sloping beaks and upright posture, give them the most humanesque appearance of any bird. Because owls' eyes are tube-shaped rather than round, they remain nearly immobile within their sockets. These birds must weave and tilt and turn their heads—sometimes as much as 270 degrees—to look around or behind them. Their visual sensitivity and acuity allow them to see well in conditions of extremely low light, perfect for hunting in the evenings and early mornings. It turns out owls aren't strictly nocturnal; most are crepuscular—active at dawn and dusk.

Their brilliant eyesight is matched—if not exceeded—by their pristine hearing. Rather than the small holes that serve as ears in most bird species, owls have "half-moon-shaped vertical slits, nearly as deep as the head itself."[1] Many owls' ear openings are asymmetrical, aiding their powers of prey detection and location pinpointing to within a hairsbreadth. Great Gray, Long-eared, and American Barn Owls can "locate invisible small mammals from the air" while those animals—usually rodents—are traveling under snow cover and then "catch them blindly by pouncing on the correct spot below the snow surface."[2] Anyone who's walked in a winter wonderland, marveling at its fluffy, snow-covered silences, can imagine how imperceptibly muffled a mouse tunneling through a drift would sound. Owls can hear noises just a tick above the sound of quietness itself.

In contrast to their solitary reputations, a few owl species are quite sociable. Burrowing Owls raise their babies in loose colonies. Most others raise their young in male-female, or occasionally male-female-female, pairings and share hunting grounds with hawks, sometimes even handing off a well-suited perch to a companionable raptor during the day before taking it back for the hours between dusk and dawn.

Owls are common throughout the world, found everywhere but the polar ice caps and a few isolated, remote islands. With over two hundred species total, owls hold a good share of whimsical names, including the Elf Owl, Spectacled Owl, and Laughing Owl. A group of owls is called a parliament, a congress, a wisdom, a hooting, or a stare.

They are silent, otherworldly killers. They swoop down on their prey in the dwindling light of dusk or the pitch-dark of night or the gray shades of morning, and for the vole or the gopher, the mouse or the rabbit, there is nothing but death. The end of the world in an instant, a neck snapped, blood drained into the soil. It is T. S. Eliot's apocalyptic finale, the world that ends "not with a bang, but a whimper."[3]

For us, too, the end will come. Will it be silent or end in a cacophony of shrieks and screams? The end somehow seems impossible—a hundred thousand years away—and also imminent, lurking at every conference table of posturing politicians. It sounds laughable and deadly serious at the same time. The end of the world? Surely we jest. We make jokes because to take it earnestly would require a level of self-reflection we do not often wish to embrace.

But wait. Stop. Listen. Underneath all the fear is a beating heart, not of a deadly owl but of a God who will one day say *enough*. This is not terror, but grace.

I read and read and read about owls but have yet to see one in the wild. This is immensely frustrating, as I am certain I've hiked past easily fifty owls. Despite my owling books telling me things like, "Almost anywhere you go in the world you can find an owl, if you know where to look," I have not found this to be the case. I know *where* to look—tall evergreens, the holes in hollow trees, high, scrubby brush—and *when*—twilight, evening, or early morning—but still I come up owlless. I search the forest floor for owl pellets, the regurgitated, hairy chunks of indigestible animal parts like skulls and spines and claws, and the tree trunks for white swaths of droppings, but they remain hidden. Owls' proclivities for camouflage, combined with my own impatience in standing still for long are an impossible combination. I feel like Michael Scott yelling about turtles: *Where are the owls?!*

Occasionally a friend or neighbor will call to tell me there's an owl in their yard, on their fence, in their canyon, and I hop in my car to go and see, but always the owl has moved on by the time I've arrived. One evening I was late for dinner because I kept hearing what I was convinced was a Great Horned Owl at a local park—and the sound ID on my birding app confirmed it!—but my binocular search of each tall pine came up short.

As a teenager, I'd prayed that Jesus wouldn't return until I fell in love. That requirement satisfied, now I didn't want the world to end before I saw an owl. There will be owls in the eschaton, I am certain of it, but also, I want to see one in this life. You can imagine my unfettered delight when, the summer I turned forty, Daryl gave me a gift.

"Get in the car," he said. "I'm taking you to meet an owl for your birthday."

In Wisconsin, I pick up my rental car and drive the hour and a half to my grandparents' home in the northern forests, nestled on Lower Kaubeshine Lake and nearly unchanged in every way since my last visit years ago, except there's more religious art now. Lots more.

Grandma and I embrace at the front door. She is exactly as I remember her, smelling freshly of soap, clean and airy, thin and sturdy in my arms. She wears her gray hair in the same Katherine Hepburn-style pin curls I watched her carefully arrange when I was a girl, coiling freshly-washed strands against her head with two crossed bobby pins until they dried, when she would finger-comb them loose.

She offers me food and drink, but it is late. I am hungry most for sleep, weary from the road, from running and driving and trying to nap while upright and tilted slightly forward (why are airplane seats *like* that?), so after initial pleasantries and hugs and "How are you doings," I put on my pajamas and brush my teeth and rinse the airplane off my face. I am about to call out to ask where she'd like me to sleep when something—I might even call it the Holy Spirit—gives me pause. The draw to introvert—to pause in stillness after a day of travel and close proximity to other people—is strong. Grandpa and I have always had that in common. But Grandma has stories to share, I can sense it, so I slip a hoodie over my pajamas and go back to the living room to listen and learn and honor.

"Have you seen any new birds in your yard?" I ask. Grandma and I sit at the darkened picture window and she tells me about the turkey that perched on her porch railing last week, then about her beloved Catholic church and favorite priest—Father Maria Joseph. I listen to stories of her volunteer work for hospice, about the last vestiges of snow that are holding on with an icy grip, about her best friend, Marge, who died last year.

Then she tells me the story of Grandpa's fall, how long he was on the floor. She shows me how she kept him comfortable with cushions and fed him snacks to stabilize his blood sugar while they waited for help to arrive.

"Don't get old," she tells me. "It's the pits."

Then she gives me a tour of her new iconography and statues, including a one-armed Saint Francis perched atop a bureau—the patron saint of animals, who is said to have preached even to the birds.

"Can you believe someone was going to just throw him out?" she asks, tsking. My grandmother is a champion tsker. "When people die, their families put these things out with the trash, but I can't bear to see them thrown out."

She has always gravitated to those on the margins—children, the elderly, the misfits, the dying. As a young girl I begged to visit her as often as possible, to stay overnight and have special time, just the two of us, free from the pull of my younger sisters. I felt so important at her house, not one of a pack of children, but singled out for care, my thoughts as valuable as any adult's. Grandma and I would lie on our backs atop the quilt on her bed, staring at the slanted, stippled ceiling while she told me stories about any animal I could name. I tried to stump her—surely she didn't know any stories about an *octopus!*—but she always came through. She believed popcorn and Hershey's chocolate bars could be an acceptable dinner and let me play her aging Nintendo until my thumbs bled.

I had not realized that her compassion for those on the edges extended to discarded relics as well, but it is clear from her bedroom that Catholic paraphernalia is being welcomed by the boxload. Grandma introduces me to bedazzled Jesus and life-size woven Mary and a massive photocopy of the Shroud of Turin.

"You can sleep here," she says, gesturing to a twin bed positioned between a framed icon of Mary, her hands gesturing to her glowing, sacred heart, and one of a haloed Jesus, his heart dripping with blood as he stands surrounded by pink roses and silver sequins, a cross between Orlando Bloom and Elvis. Despite my protestations—there's a second bed, after all—she insists on taking the couch in the living room.

"I don't sleep anyway," she says. "Not really."

Together we make a plan for the morning—breakfast, with coffee for me and hot chocolate for her. (She's given up coffee for Lent, and sweets, too, except hot chocolate doesn't count. I'd also forgotten about her logic, the syllogisms all her own.) Then we will head to the hospital to speak with Grandpa about which rehabilitation facility will be the best fit.

"He wants to come home," she says, folding her hands atop the lacquered black table that's sat here beside her picture window as far back as I can remember. The dark woods stretch out before us, parallel rows of towering white pines. They lead my eye out into the night, to the inky black lake where the lawn ends just beyond.

"I can't lift him," she says, echoing a plight I've heard from so many wives over the years as their husbands' health began to fail. The height and strength that first sparked romantic interest turns to burden in days of illness. My grandfather is not large, but my grandmother is built like a hummingbird. She looks out the window, into the darkness. "To come home, he will need to get stronger."

People lose their cool about the end times. They stand on street corners and put up billboards and claim secret knowledge of dates and times and locations. It isn't uncommon for me to receive phone calls at church from concerned people with no ties to our congregation who simply want us to know that everything is about to *end*—for reals this time—so we can *get ready*. Whether it's right-wing doomsayers or left-wing climate cynics, a lot of people are convinced we're on a fast train to Armageddon.

In *Art and Faith,* Makoto Fujimura describes this impulse to run to apocalyptic thinking: "Christian imagination today obsesses over the End rather than scanning for the New Creation in our midst."[4] Though the Scriptures spare no ink when it comes to describing the end of the world—we read it in Daniel and the Prophets, in Matthew, in Peter and Thessalonians and Revelation— their prescriptions never include fear but instead simply preparedness. We are to be watchful, not paranoid. Awake, not anxious. The coming of the Lord will arrive suddenly, Paul tells the Thessalonians, "as labor pains on a pregnant woman."[5] But here's the thing about labor pains—they may begin without much warning, but by the time they hit there's usually been months to prepare. The baby may arrive suddenly, but we can calmly and methodically get the nursery ready well ahead of time.

In the past, when friends and neighbors and congregants voiced their terror at the end of the world, I used to redirect with perhaps a sliver of unintended condescension. I'd point them to Scriptures about God's providence and care, remind them of Jesus' words that no one knows the day or hour of the end of the world and anyway, it has always been right on the horizon. We can't stave it off or bring it about any sooner. All we can attend to in this moment is how we choose to live *now.*

But post-pandemic I find my own dream life interrupted by the apocalyptic more often than not. I wake in a cold sweat about the price of groceries, the threat of nuclear powers, school violence and street violence and the quiet desperation I glimpse in the eyes of my neighbors, my congregants, myself. I wake to ash raining on my car and air too clogged with wildfire smoke for my children to take a deep breath. I weigh the trauma of allowing them to participate in active shooter drills at their schools against their unpreparedness should they need to know which cabinet to hide in from a monster.

One Saturday night I dreamed that someone moved the church's Communion table, leaving the bread and juice on a shoddy card table shoved to the side of the worship space.

"Who did this?" I asked, turning to see only empty pews. "Has church started?" I called out, my voice echoing in the cavernous space.

"It's started," a voice rang out, "but no one is here."

I woke gasping and drenched in sweat, wanting to crawl into the arms of Jesus, to turn off the news and take a few deep breaths and point all of us toward the trees.

Look up, I'd say. *Look at the birds.*

Daryl and I pull the car up to a sprawling compound in Ramona that looks like part petting zoo, part dusty villa. He parks and we're summoned over to a set of small, low buildings—sheds really—each bordered by a room-sized cage.

"I'm Terry," says an older woman with long, gray-blonde hair. "This is Kevin," she gestures to a man in his midthirties. Both are clad in typical naturalist gear—earth tone pants, sturdy shoes, slightly worn crew-neck T-shirts. They hand us a waiver that says, in essence, we won't sue them if an owl claws our eyeballs out. It's California: people are litigious about things like that. Also, an owl *could* technically claw our eyeballs out. It's not an impossible scenario. We sign and hand back the clipboard and Terry says, "Well, now that's done. Would you like to meet an owl?"

I am suddenly aware of every leaf and gnat and ray of sun, awake down to my marrow. *This is happening.*

Terry slips inside a shed and comes back with an exquisite, cinnamon-and-white feathered Barn Owl. "This is Moonshine," she says. I squeak out a breath.

"She's beautiful," I say. Moonshine is two years old and fifteen inches tall. Her apple-shaped face is concave, with bright white feathers surrounding round, black eyes and a hooked, light pink beak. She eyes us sleepily, more doe than raptor. Terry and Kevin fill us with all the owl wisdom they have to offer, talons and molting and grooming, the dangers of rat poison, the nesting cycle. They tell us where one can purchase food for owls—Rodents Pro—and what permits are required for raising exotic birds—quite a few. I've already died and gone to bird-nerd heaven when Terry gestures to a left-handed leather glove lying on the table between us.

"Would you like to hold her?" she asks.

The bird hops gingerly onto my glove. She weighs just over a pound. Up close I can see the minute details of her feathers, not just cinnamon but umber and charcoal and ecru and taupe, each a universe of constellated color. The delicate white feathers around her face are intricate as snowflakes. Myth and metaphor surround owls in abundance, and Barn Owls are one reason why. Their white faces nearly glow in the fading light of dusk, and their calls— Moonshine rewards me with a singular *screeeeeeeee!*—are eerie even in daylight.

That's my nightmare, a friend responds when I text him a picture of Moonshine. *No thank you.*

Terry then brings out Hensen, an enormous Eurasian Eagle-owl. At six pounds and over two feet tall, Hensen looks like a linebacker but, according to Kevin, is really just a surly teenage girl.

"She's six years old," he says. "That's adolescence for this type of owl." Hensen's eyes are flat orange disks, her ear tufts puffed and straight. Owls hunt silently and normally kill their larger prey with a glide-and-strike, seizing them around the neck or spine area with reflexive strength and razor-sharp talons. Hensen's talons can squeeze six hundred pounds per square inch, enough to easily snap an adult man's arm in two. Due to permit issues, we can't hold Hensen. Due to everything else, I'm glad it isn't on offer.

We were promised two owls, but as Terry prepares Hensen to return to her digs, she looks over her shoulder and pauses. "Would you like to meet one more?"

Be still my heart.

Kevin emerges with a tiny Eastern Screech Owl no bigger than a guinea pig. Owlexander the Great is mid-molt, his variegated gray feathers shaggy as a Muppet in the rain, his sage-green eyes round and blinking off-kilter, one and then, a long few seconds later, the other.

"He is not at his prettiest right now," Terry tells us, but the bedraggled vulnerability of this impossibly tiny bird of prey is spellbinding. He is glorious in his own way, with his miniature talons and delicate curved beak, stuck for the moment between scruffy pinfeathers and full matte plumage. I love him, too.

"That one looks like he is raising teenagers," a friend quips when I post a video to my social media. Eastern screech owls camouflage seamlessly into tree bark, their diminutive size allowing them to blend into the forest like the morning mist.

"No wonder I have trouble finding owls," I say, watching this frazzled, alien creature blink one eye and stare, blink the other and stare.

"They are hard to spot," says Kevin. "But keep at it. You will learn how to see."

A little art piece hangs above my writing desk with a birding verse from Matthew. *Look at the birds*, it reminds me. *Your heavenly Father feeds them.* It features a watercolor Blue Jay, a bird I chose in part because it's grumpy, vocal, and territorial. The jay reminds me that God cares for us not because we are inherently delightful or well-behaved or even trying very hard, but because of who God is. This is where I hang my apocalyptic hope: not that I'll finally get it all correct or figured out or finally crack the code into living the life I aspire to live—one that's good and kind, that is, not the kind of consumerist aspiration of washboard abs or a nice leather handbag. My hope rests on the one who feeds the cranky Blue Jays, too.

Most pastors have stories about members of their communities who went a little too far down the rabbit hole of eschatology. It's a natural path to take when we're anxious. Also, it makes more than a little bit of sense if you've spent any time at all in Revelation. That book is intense and not easy to parse, even for scholars and theologians. Just the descriptions of the angels—the good guys!— are enough to make us shudder. Jesus might be the Lamb of God, but he doesn't show up cute and cuddly; instead he looks as though he's been slain. It's a book of pestilence and plague, despair and darkness, brimstone and fire. Before the dawn comes a devastating, lengthy, backbreaking night. Like an owl, the end strikes silently, unexpectedly, bringing us to a bloody conclusion.

The macabre quality of Revelation is a word to us in and of itself. So often we want our Jesus meek and mild, tidy and tender. We want our lives that way, too. But that is rarely the way they end up.

As a child I wanted to become a veterinarian because I loved animals and adored the entire James Herriot series. It was all so lovely and helpful. Named after hymns, even! *All Creatures Great and*

Small, All Things Wise and Wonderful. I turned the pages and imagined myself in a white coat delivering news to a desperate family that their beloved dog would pull through, their cat's leg would heal, their horse would rally.

Then my parents arranged for me to shadow our local veterinarian for a day, part of a homeschooling unit on career exploration. Within the first half hour at the clinic, the vet, a thin, humorless man with a meticulously trimmed beard, sliced open a German shepherd on his operating table, and I passed out cold. Prepared for literary tidiness, I got blood and feces and the smell of wet dog. I realized I loved reading about veterinary medicine but was ill-equipped to *do* it.

The same is true of many a seminary student, heading to the pastorate with abundant goodwill and love for humanity but a real distaste for the messiness of actual people. It's easy to have good feelies about the masses until the board chair resigns before a major meeting because he's angry at another board member but won't talk about it because *she knows what she did.*

It also doesn't help that ministry is just so very ordinary. It's that fact more than anything that burns so many of us out. It isn't the funeral sermon or the Communion service or the Sunday school lesson that exhausts—here we can point to big, true, glorious things. It is the sixty-seventh committee meeting and the ongoing rivalry over Christmas decorations and the typo in the bulletin circled in red pen and stuffed into our mailbox. Most ministry professionals enter the vocation because somewhere along the journey God gripped their soul with the hope of transcendence, but much of ministry is pulling weeds and tilling soil and waiting, waiting, waiting for a tiny tendril of transformation to sprout up from its depths. We want to proclaim glory when most people just want lunch. If we're honest, we usually just want lunch, too.

In light of all this apocalyptic anxiety, a good meal probably wouldn't be a bad place to start. It's where we're destined to end, after all, at the wedding supper of the Lamb.

Revelation is in the canon for a reason, not to mention the many other Scriptures that point us toward the end of days, but there are parallel risks to learning about the end of the world. The first is that we'll become obsessive, giving it too much time and attention to the neglect of the Bible's full arc. People in this camp are frequently tempted to read things into the text that simply aren't there. My sisters had the pants scared off them at church camp one summer when their program leader started ranting about how "they've found the red heifer in Israel and that means the end is near!" He never explained who *they* were or the significance of the red heifer, but my sisters spent the rest of his talk trying to slowly edge their way out the door.

The second risk is that we'll ignore it altogether. In the 1980s and '90s evangelicals got themselves in quite a bit of eco-trouble by focusing on souls at the expense of the planet. (This is a problem we're still untangling today.) *Why should we care for the earth if it's all going to burn anyway?* the argument went. It has taken patient work by activists and theologians and biblical scholars to help reorient us as stewards of God's good creation rather than abusers of it.

Recently, the end of the world came for a dear man in our church who had grown even wiser and kinder with age. He died how he lived—with dignity and grace. His end times were marked not by angels with four faces and four wings but by a beeping monitor above a hospital bed and a calm assurance that he would be met by the love of the Savior he'd faithfully followed for more than three-quarters of a century.

Daryl got a text with the news and we wept together. Daryl had been at his hospital bedside less than an hour before. No one tells you that the longer you pastor in one place, the heavier the weight of grief becomes. Our first years in ministry we buried acquaintances and congregants. Now we bury friends.

I found a photograph of our youngest child, Felicity, then just two and a half years old, sharing a donut with this man on the church patio one Sunday morning, his blue walker clearly in view. He'd carefully settled at a table with two chairs—one for him, one for his wife—when Felicity bounded over and plopped down, claiming one for herself.

"I'm sorry!" I said, trying to scoot her away.

"This is wonderful," he said, waving me off as Felicity grinned, her dimples coated in chocolate frosting.

Illness had bowed him low, his once regal posture stooped and trembling. To be with him so close to the moment of death was a profound gift to Daryl, a pastoral moment of being invited into a thin place. For just a moment, the barrier between heaven and earth blurred and the sacred reached right down to brush his lips with a coal. The things we witness. The stories we hold. The more years I serve in ministry, the more I am in awe of the wingbeat of the Spirit in and through all things.

The line between life and death is fine as the edge of a feather.

In Wisconsin, I wake early and head to the shower, rinsing off yesterday's travels. In the kitchen, Grandma is brewing coffee and has set out a huge array of fruit and eggs, gluten-free donuts and bread and prepackaged smoothies that aren't easy to find this far north.

"I don't know what you like," she said, "but you can prepare whatever looks good to you."

"Where did you *get* all of this?" I ask. "I couldn't eat this much food if I stayed for a month!"

"Your parents brought it over," she says.

I've arrived with a backpack full of snacks, not wanting to inconvenience anyone with my persistent and obnoxious dietary issues, but also forgetting how much food represents love here in the Midwest. Our unofficial regional motto is: *we will overfeed you or die trying.* I sip my coffee, dark and rich and smooth.

"What is this?" I ask, picturing a specialty blend. "It's really good." She opens a cabinet to reveal a giant blue plastic tub.

"Maxwell House?" she says. Exhaustion does wonders for the palate.

I am scrambling an egg—Grandma doesn't want one; she is busy sipping what smells like a hot cup of vinegar (and which is, I discover on closer inspection, exactly that) when her phone rings.

"It's the doctor," she says. "I'll put it on speaker."

The doctor slowly unpacks the story of the previous twelve hours.

"I'm afraid John really took a turn last night," he begins. "I am so very sorry, but I do not think rehabilitation will be possible."

I see Grandma receive this information one word at a time, assimilating knowledge that she's helped countless families understand during her hospice years. She knows what he is likely to say next. We stand in silence and wait for it to come.

"It looks like we are nearing the end," says the doctor. "If you have people to call who would like to come, I would call them soon."

She thanks him and turns toward the window.

6

DAILINESS

HOUSE FINCHES

How we spend our days is, of course,
how we spend our lives.

Annie Dillard

TWO BIRD FEEDERS HANG IN our backyard, gifts from a friend. Sparrows jockey for position, Mourning Doves and a Rock Pigeon waiting on the ground for seeds knocked loose in the fray. We see the occasional House Wren and Hooded Oriole and Black Grosbeak, too, perched in neighboring trees, watching the other birds come and go. Crows hang out on the stone wall. The mockingbird is a noisy fixture. But mostly we have daily visits from our House Finches.

There are at least a dozen with their subtly forked tails, heavy beaks, and chipper songs. The call of a House Finch borders on stereotypical: *Cheep! Cheep, cheep, CHEEP!* My friend Mark calls their songs a curlicue, an apt description with the way their twittering ends on an uptilt. Nearly every birding book attempts to write out birdcalls, for better ease of identification, but putting text to an avian song is like trying to paint a flavor. Does the Common Yellow-throat say *ta-wicha, ta-wicha, ta-wicha* or *Wichita-Wichita-Wichita* or *too-witchy, too-witchy, too-witchy*? And if you've never heard one before, can you really pick it out in the tall grass because of a few letters on a page? Some birds are mimics. Others repeat the same few notes. Still, there's charm in trying to put words to avian song, and I love guidebook authors for how they keep trying.

For those seeking to identify and remember birds, it does help to pair their calls with memorable words or phrases or everyday antiphons. Birders adopt the song terminology of their favorite authors or podcasters, or else come up with our own. To me, the call of the California Towhee sounds like a smoke alarm that's drained its batteries. The Allen's Hummingbird speaks in a tiny, raspy scold. The House Finches cheep in curlicues as they maneuver for seeds. Until spring, that is, when their songs change.

In the early morning, the northern Wisconsin woods are frosty and muddy and wet, with a gray that soaks right down to the bones. Dormant grasses long buried under snowfall are just beginning to emerge, soggy and brown. Patches of dirty snow remain, and the gravel road leading into town from Grandma's house is deeply rutted. We drive through Hazelhurst, passing metal pole buildings and tourist attractions and the Christmas Chalet—a big slate-blue building selling seasonal kitsch I always begged to visit as a kid. We pass a school bus and suddenly I remember that it's Tuesday. School is in session. Two thousand miles away, Daryl is getting our children ready, stuffing backpacks with lunches and homework and trying to convince our youngest to let him brush her hair.

I pull into the hospital parking lot behind Grandma's Jeep and look around for a pay station before remembering that this is the rural Midwest, where parking is always free. The hospital is new, sprung from the gravelly soil in the years since I last visited, shiny and spacious and pristine. We take the elevator up and walk to Grandpa's room—private, with a big window facing the forest— and suddenly I am grateful for God's kindness in these small touches. The room isn't shared. The room isn't shabby. The room lets in the light of the day, gray as that light might be. In the bed at the room's center, Grandpa is sleeping.

Grandma moves to his bedside. His face is covered by a transparent oxygen mask and his mouth is open in sleep, his brow furrowed. He's always been lean, but in his later, even leaner years, I've never seen him without layers of shirts—long-sleeved green or gray cotton topped with a sweatshirt or a flannel or both. Now, in this thin hospital gown, I can see the waxy yellow skin over his clavicle, the veins crossing from his neck to his shoulder. His wrists are covered in plastic bands—a purple DNR, a yellow fall risk, a white hospital admission bracelet. His hair is gray and wispy. He looks somehow smaller, in the way people do when pain tends to crouch them inward. He looks somehow larger, too, in the way the specter of death can expand to fill a room. He looks just like my grandfather and nothing at all like him. I see the three of us tumbling through a doorway into the thin places, like Alice down the rabbit hole.

"I'm here, John," Grandma says. She squeezes his shoulder. I'm on my way to join her at his bedside when a nurse slips in through the door. She introduces herself as Beth, the one who'll be on Grandpa's case throughout the day, and it becomes clear within seconds that she is a woman of great proficiency and practical goodness. She tiptoes around the news from last night, speaking at length about kidney function and fluid in the lung, until I break in gently to tell her my grandmother is a hospice volunteer and I'm a pastor.

"We aren't squeamish," I tell her. "You can be straight with us."

She takes a breath.

"I think it will be soon," she says. "I think you should tell people to come, if they want to say goodbye."

Beth heads back out on her rounds while Grandma pulls a phone from her pocket and moves into the hallway. Grandpa and I are, for the moment, alone. I suspect that these moments of intimacy without spectators will be a rare gift, and I'm thankful. Unless I'm working from prepared remarks, I don't do well with an audience. I sit down in a folding chair at Grandpa's bedside.

"Grandpa, it's Courtney," I say. "I came from California. I'm here and I love you."

His eyelids flutter but remain closed.

I reach for his hand, but he jerks it away—reflex or sleep motion or perhaps a little frustration that it took him dying for me to visit for the first time in all these years. I lay a hand gently on his arm and he lets it stay. We sit together in the weak light of the cloud-filtered morning, grandfather and oldest grandchild, separated by almost exactly fifty years and the gray plastic railing of a hospital bed. I watch his chest rise and fall gently with his breaths and see decades expand and compress. He was a baby, once. His hands held my mother as a baby and then me and then my children. I have so much I want to say, but my grandfather has never been one for sentimentality or many words, and anyway, he isn't awake. So I sit and watch.

I knew I was coming to say goodbye.

I didn't know I would be bearing witness to his final hours.

When I ask a couple who's been together fifty, sixty years what their secret is, most often they'll give me a bemused sort of smile and nonanswer.

"Oh, just care for each other."

"We try to be kind."

"I say that I love her every day, and she says it back."

Perhaps it is impossible to describe the intangibles that make a good and lasting partnership. We have to resort to explaining via sweeping generalities like *love* and *patience* and *kindness*.

In spring, House Finches are looking for partners, for their One True Love™ for at least a few weeks of mating and nest-building and egg-laying. They turn into loud little things, their usual short calls bursting into lengthy songs. It's speedy gibberish that ends on an upturn, like a happy question: *Chatterchatterchatterchatterchatter . . . okaaaaaay?* Their spring is loquacious; their love letters prolific. They are courting, twitterpated, head over heels.

In the spring of our relationship, Daryl and I wrote dozens of letters, first mailed to our college post office boxes and then across the country as we took our first burgeoning steps at independent adulthood—he in Boston, I in Colorado. He studied theological German at Harvard and I interned at a rock-climbing magazine, both of us running hard and fast on tracks for careers we would eventually set aside to step into pastoral ministry. We were young and ambitious, singing rapid-fire to one another through pen and page. There were so many questions to ask. There was so much to say.

If our marriage were a person, it'd be in driver's ed now, aged sixteen years. We've become the House Finches of late summer, their calls worn down by the relentless heat and the raising of young until most of what they have to say to one another can be summed up in familiar chirrups of sameness. I used to fear this season, the shine of a marriage all worn off. It seemed sad, somehow, to develop so much shorthand that words would often not even be necessary, because all could be communicated with a heavy sigh or a wry smile or a nod toward the dishwasher. Our spring plumage has faded; the eggs have hatched. This could be a season where the thrill is gone, and there are days I look for signs of malaise and apathy, the settled sadnesses of middle age.

But instead I find that shabby chic is its own glory. We revel in intangibles as hard to put into words as the call of a bird—things like trust and stability and faithfulness and care. To grow old with someone does not have to be, as I once feared, rote or boring or filled with half-buried resentments. It can be a miraculous thing, a House Finch returning to the feeder again and again and again, weary from the flight but waiting a holy wingbeat so his partner can eat first. It's more miraculous still when this kindness is extended not just one time but ten thousand.

Alice Walker once quipped that women "should have children— assuming this is of interest to them—but only one."[1] When asked to elaborate, she replied, "Because with one you can move. With more than one you're a sitting duck." It is easy to disdain and despair the common tasks of daily life—at some point, most movers and shakers would argue, the toilet scrubbing and diaper changing and grocery shopping must be outsourced so we have time for more important things.

I'm all for saving time. One of the best investments we've made in our family life of two-working-parents-plus-a-writing-career was to hire a cleaning service to come twice a month as soon as we could afford it. We roll through the drive-through more than most nutritionists would advise. We are big fans of nonfussy clothing—wash it, dry it, wear it. In my mind, a label that reads "Dry clean only" might as well say "Do not purchase." Don't even get me started on ironing.

Even so, I wonder whether the work we're so quick to cast aside—the everyday dishes and linens and crumbs spilled on the carpet—is part of God's invitation to holiness. I wonder if the relentless *drip, drip, drip* of daily tasks is divinely designed to help wear down our sharper edges. I wonder how much of the ordinary is quiet grace in disguise.

I'm hanging artwork the children have drawn for Grandpa on the wall in front of his bed when Grandma returns.

"They're all going to come," she says, her phone in her hand. "Your parents and sisters are on their way, and Johnny and Eileen and the boys are going to come soon, too."

My grandparents have two children—my mom, the eldest, and my Uncle John, who lives with his wife in the Chicago suburbs. My cousins, two boys, are fifteen and sixteen years younger than I am, both recent college graduates living in the Midwest. My sisters, Caitlyn and Caroline, have driven from their homes and families in Minnesota to spend these days supporting my parents. Somehow we've all sensed the urgency. In a few hours we will all be together again at the same time, a first since the pandemic began.

"Do you want a few moments?" I ask my grandmother.

"Okay," she says. "Okay."

She sits, and I gently scratch between her shoulder blades, tracing circles on her heavy fleece jacket. This was the same gesture of love and comfort she used to help me fall asleep when I'd visit her as a young girl. *Grumples,* she called it. She sighs.

"I'll give you an hour to stop that," she says, leaning into my hand.

I continue a little longer, hug her gently, then turn to the door. "I'll be back in a few minutes," I say, my eyes brimming.

They've been married sixty-four years.

The bulk of the church calendar is dedicated to Ordinary Time—the weeks and months that stitch together the spaces between the holy seasons of Advent and Lent. After Eastertide comes Pentecost Sunday—the day we remember the coming of the Holy Spirit in tongues—*flames!*—of fire in the book of Acts. Then no more liturgical confetti cannons for months until we take the turn toward Advent once again. The one time we preached on the same book of the Bible for the entire season of Ordinary Time, people begged for something—anything—new. The daily grind can wear us down to a fine powder, ready to blow away in a breath. But the color of Ordinary Time isn't gray—it's green. The color of growth, of lush meadows and mossy forests and boggy wetlands pulsating with life. Our lives are built out of the blocks of our ordinary days. A hundred sunrises, a thousand dinners, a million baskets of laundry. Backyard birds so common to residential areas they have the very word in their names: House Sparrow. House Wren. House Finch. The same song sung day after day after day.

I grew up where House Finches and Wrens were rare. It was Black-capped Chickadees we witnessed in abundance, prevalent as pine trees in the northern Wisconsin forests. They blended into the expected landscape like grass or snow or gravel.

"Oh, it's just a chickadee," my sisters and I would say anytime we could be persuaded to glance at the feeder my mother hung from the eaves. To us they were nothing special.

There is a cross-country ski trail near my childhood home that leads to a little wooden warming hut in the forest. If you fill your palm with sunflower seeds and sit very quietly for a few moments, chickadees will come and take seeds from your hand. The first time one landed on my thumb, its weight only a breath, its toes gripping with tiny black nails, I startled, launching my handful of black seeds—and the poor, disgruntled bird—into the air. But chickadees are very forgiving, and with attention to my breathing, I readied myself for its return.

A chickadee eyed me from a low-hanging pine bough for a moment, deciding whether my waxy seeds were worth the risk. Its body looked round and fat, its winter feathers fluffed for warmth. As I watched the first bird, another swooped down from behind me to perch on my thumb. This time, I held still. It inspected my offerings before bending to snatch a seed in its pointed black beak. Another joined it and chose a seed for herself, then both flew off.

I sat until my hand grew numb with cold, holding feathered miracles and listening to their calls—*chickadee-dee-dee, chickadeeeeee.* There are thousands upon thousands of these black-capped songbirds in the Midwest. They are common. Ordinary. But that doesn't lessen their magic.

These are the true miracles—wiping the nose of the child for the hundredth time, forgiving the careless word even while suspecting another may come on its heels, showing up once more to the pew, kneeling down again and again and again, waiting for God to speak. Comedian Jim Gaffigan jokes of Catholic Mass that if you haven't been in a while, "it's still going on."[2] This is the truest thing I know about Jesus, the reason I became a pastor all those years ago. The world may froth and spin, storm and steam. Fads and flavors will come and go. Wars and revolutions will rise and die. Nations will rage, as the psalmist says, and the people plot in vain. Unpredictability is often the order of the day. Yet the truest things of all will keep on until the very end. Through it all, God remains.

In college I dated a boy who always had a new idea, a plan, an adrenaline-fueled escapade. I talked him out of crab fishing in Alaska one summer—sure, it paid well, but also he might die—but couldn't dissuade him from biking the entire western coast of the United States instead.

"Will you call me sometimes?" I asked.

"Well," he paused, "I don't know how often we'll be near phones."

It was then I realized I didn't want to marry exciting. I wanted to marry stable. Faithful. Life hands us enough chaos on its own.

On Easter Sunday and Christmas Eve and Mother's Day, our church fills to bursting. Some Sundays in Ordinary Time it sits nearly empty. And still, the Spirit of God is hovering—*brooding*, the Hebrew says—over the waters. The House Finch is asking her question. The chickadee is forgiving.

I am a witness to the ordinary transcendence God places before me. And so are you, to yours.

I can't decide whether I should wake Grandpa or just sit quietly beside him. Grandma is back out in the hallway, taking a moment for herself, and I can feel the time slipping through my fingers. Soon the room will be crowded. I sit in the chair and watch the seconds tick away.

Suddenly I remember visiting my great-grandmother at her home in Chicago a decade and a half earlier, bringing her a slice of cream cake from her favorite bakery. I let myself in with my key, the one a great-uncle had pressed into my hand with tender urgency months before, grateful to have a capable graduate student living just blocks away from the family matriarch, able to check in on her in an emergency. I stepped softly on the burgundy-carpeted stairs that wound up to her dining room.

"Gram?" I shouted. Her hearing had been gone for years, and her hearing aids were rarely in her ears. I didn't want to startle her. She'd been mugged in her alleyway a few years back, thrown to the ground so the assailant could flee with her purse, and it had made her skittish.

"Gram? Are you here? It's Courtney!"

Her bedroom at the front of the house overlooked Cornelia Street in Chicago's Lakewood neighborhood, just a few blocks from the bustle of Wrigley Field. I gently pushed open the door. She was sitting upright in a chair, facing the window, wearing her usual flowered nightgown and housecoat. Her hands lay gently folded in her lap in a beam of sun, a rosary draped across her fingers. She was sleeping.

I returned to the dining room and wrote her a note, leaving it tucked underneath the slice of cake, a surprise for whenever she woke up.

I later learned she was heartbroken I hadn't roused her.

"I have my whole life to sleep," she had said. "It's all I do. I barely see you."

Spurred on by the ghost of Great-Grandmother Past, I try to squeeze Grandpa's hand again, to gently discern if he wants to be awake, but it's lodged underneath his covers.

"Grandpa?" I say softly. "It's Courtney. I'm here."

He shifts and grunts.

"I love you, Grandpa," I say. "Daryl and the kids love you."

A flood comes now. I lean in and say all the things I'd hoped I would have the chance to say, all the things that sound like clichés until the moment those big, broad words are all we have left, because anything narrower won't encompass the depth of our feelings on the edge of eternity. I say thank you and I love you and I tell him that I'm so glad he is my grandfather. I thank him for teaching me to love the outdoors, to not be afraid of silence, to appreciate the gifts of birds and cats and dogs. I tell him that Daryl sends his love. I tell him that we will take care of Grandma.

Then I describe each of our children to him, grandkids he hasn't hugged in person for two long pandemic years and will now never meet again in this life.

"I want to tell you about the kids, Grandpa. They are growing up so well and I see you in each of them. Lincoln is so smart; he has this analytic brain and he loves math and equations and science and thinks so deeply about everything. And Wilson! Wilson is our engineer. Maybe he'll grow up to be one just like you. He's fascinated by how things work and is always building, building, building. He creates a fort every single day, and he has this tender heart that loves animals and soft things. And Felicity, oh Grandpa, you would love Felicity. She has big dimples and a huge personality and she doesn't miss a thing. She's incredibly observant and silly and doesn't take any nonsense from anybody. They each have your blue eyes, Grandpa, and your blonde hair."

I pause to wipe the tears cascading down my face. His brow furrows more deeply; I can see his eyes moving beneath his eyelids.

"I wanted to tell you what a wonderful grandpa you've always been to me. I will carry the memories with me forever of sitting with you by the lake and watching the birds and going fishing. I'm so sorry I haven't been to visit you for so long. I'm here now, and I love you. I will always love you."

He grimaces in pain. I scramble for his nurse call button.

7

———

BROKENNESS AND SIN

HUMMINGBIRDS

———

The greatest of all faults is
to be conscious of none.

THOMAS CARLYLE

To BECOME A BIRDER IS to have your heart broken again and again. Because birding is an exercise in attentiveness, stillness, and observation, those who watch birds tune in to more than just the winged creatures themselves. Birders pick up on the ebb and flow of seasons and migrations, noticing patterns of weather and climate, development and decay.

Beginning to perceive that which previously went overlooked comes with hard and painful edges. Nature holds a myriad of brutalities, red indeed in tooth and claw. A fledgling tries to fly too early and plummets from the nest; a flock contracts a virus and dies horribly, dropping from the sky in singles and pairs; a hawk tears open the breast of a mated bird, leaving her partner bereft. Tuning in to the beauty and wonder of nature means we will also not escape its horrors.

But it isn't just the normal ferocities of the natural world that bring an ache. It is also the ways we ravage creation. It is difficult to get into birding without becoming an armchair ecologist. Those who spot the curve of a tail feather will also perceive hotter temperatures, unpredictable storms, spiraling wildfires, invasive species. And we will often feel isolated in our noticing. As Aldo Leopold once put it:

> One of the penalties of an ecological education is that one lives alone in a world of wounds. Much of the damage inflicted on land is quite invisible to lay[people]. An ecologist must either harden his shell and make believe that the consequences of science are none of his business, or he must be the doctor who sees the marks of death in a community that believes itself well and does not want to be told otherwise.[1]

The parallels between the grieving naturalist and the anguished prophet are many. Both plead for a change. Both hope for a turning. Both are often ignored, exiled, or worse.

In researching for this book, I quickly found myself heartsick about how many animals are teetering on the precipice of extinction and the devastating numbers of those that have already toppled over, never to be known again on this earth.

Journalist Sam Anderson chronicled the death of the last male Northern White Rhinoceros, an aged beast named Sudan, in 2020. "The day Sudan died, everything felt both monumental and ordinary," he wrote. The rhino "lay still in the dirt, thick legs folded under him, huge head tilted like a capsizing ship. . . . Every desperate measure—legal, political, scientific—had already been exhausted."[2] As the animal prepared to breathe his last, he was surrounded by caregivers, people who'd lovingly tended him in the final years of his life, witnesses to the end of the world for an entire species. Wrote Anderson, "The men scratched Sudan's rough skin, said goodbye, made promises, apologized for the sins of humanity."

Loving God's good creation is an exercise in grief.

The natural world can mirror the sorrows of the human one. My friend Gretchen watches her Minnesotan backyard each year for the return of a pair of Rose-breasted Grosbeaks. One spring, juggling homeschool lesson plans and her own writing projects, she pulled up the news to see reports of another mass shooting. She wrote:

> I shut my laptop. I can't deal with death today. I feel it too much. There are littles who need me. So, I went for a walk out to my garden, to clear my head. I found the pair of rose-breasted grosbeaks—the ones I've been waiting to come back, dead on the ground. And I cried.[3]

Opening ourselves to the wonder and beauty of creation is risky. It would be less painful—for now—to simply ignore the natural world. Or if not to ignore it outright, to tell ourselves that none of the ways it's been mistreated are our fault. After all, we didn't drive the bulldozer or poach the big game or manufacture the items that poisoned the air. The temptation to pass the responsibility for care is a powerful one. *I thank you, God, that I'm not like other men,* prayed the publican. As Dietrich Bonhoeffer put it, "Self-justification and judging others go together."[4]

But the gospel invitation is that we would allow our hearts to break over all of it—our own sin, the sin of our neighbors and community, and the systemic sin so entangled in what it means to be human that we can never fully get free. Broken hearts are tilled soil, fertile and ready for the seeds of repentance. We are summoned to take what action we can, while remembering all the while that the work—and hope—rest ultimately with the Lord. We may kneel with the White Rhino's caregivers, weeping for the sins of humanity. We can treat our woods and wilds with wisdom and compassion. And we must throw ourselves on the mercy of God, for even the best-intentioned among us cannot help but participate, knowingly or unknowingly, in systems of great evil.

In college, my friend Sara served on the board of multiple environmental organizations. She ate a vegetarian diet and lived simply so she could better support causes dear to her. One spring break she and three other friends and I left campus to drive south to Tennessee. With our car's gas tank on empty, Josh, our driver, pulled into a Shell station.

"Oh, not here," Sara whispered from the back seat. Her brand of activism was gentle steel. Josh raised an eyebrow but pulled back onto the road. A couple of miles further on, he pulled into an Exxon.

"Oh," Sara whispered. "We can't fill up at an Exxon."

Josh turned over his shoulder to stare her down.

"The Valdez, Josh!" she protested. "We can't get gas at an Exxon station!"

It slowly began to dawn on the rest of us that Sara didn't own a car.

"Sara," Josh said. "Do you want to go to Tennessee?"

She nodded.

"Then where would you like us to get gas?"

She pondered for a moment. Then she shrugged, a single tear making its way down her cheek.

None of us is unscathed by sin, but it isn't just our own personal choices that affect the state of the earth. Even when we pay particular, loving attention to the environment, living in this world entails some level of complicity—aware or unaware—with the destructive practices of communities, cultures, and corporations. Nearly two decades ago, Daryl found himself nearly paralyzed with anxiety over how and where to buy me an engagement ring. He'd read about blood diamonds—gemstones from mines in Sierra Leone and Angola where workers suffered horrific human rights abuses and the diamonds themselves funded devastating civil wars. Despite my assurances that I didn't need a diamond (or even a ring—fancy jewelry has never been my thing), he was determined to find one that was both beautiful and ethically sourced. After weeks of research, he finally made a purchase, but later returned it when the jeweler couldn't offer the promised certificate ensuring its origins.

"I didn't want the symbol of our love to also be a symbol of *death*," he said. (Yes, he is an Enneagram One.) He eventually proposed with a beautiful, simple ring featuring a lab-produced diamond and recycled gold. It cost him an extra few hundred dollars, not to mention weeks of research.

However, few of us have hours to dedicate to studying the ethical practices of each item we purchase (or the extra scratch to pay more when we're already just getting by). Free-range chickens are four times the price of cage-raised, and my kids can take down one of those at a single meal. Sometimes we just need a T-shirt or a pair of sneakers or a bunch of bananas to bring to the PTA meeting. Ethical concerns can become crippling if we let them. We can do only so much, even with infinite time and good intentions. This doesn't absolve us, but neither does it put the responsibility squarely on us to save the world. Instead we are invited to a dance from awareness to grief to working for good to trusting God with the rest, one that precedes us and will go on long after we are gone. It doesn't absolve us, but hopefully it will not permanently shatter us, either.

This dance can be an arduous one. It is always easier to numb and ignore. The death of Sudan, the last Northern White Rhino on earth, was an apocalyptic tragedy that went unnoticed by the vast majority of the world. Those who don't love don't grieve, and goodness knows we all have more than enough to grieve as it is. But closing ourselves off to creation comes with a steep cost of its own.

Those who don't love miss out on loving.

We are all here at the hospital now, my two younger sisters and my parents and my grandmother and me. We are doing the things you do in hospital rooms when death lurks at the door: sitting, waiting, making small talk, ensuring everyone gets a turn to sit in the best chair, telling stories, laughing, falling silent. My sisters have brought food—*so* much food. Caroline presses a cold brew into my hand. Caitlyn stirs a communal dish of quinoa and fruit. Several grocery bags of additional supplies sit near the door. I hand out the gifts I brought with me—chocolate and books and a sage-green dress for my mom that matches the ones Felicity and I have. My uncle is already on his way from Chicago. My aunt is gathering my cousins to bring them north.

We speak again to Nurse Beth, who is quickly becoming a friend. She tells the truth to the new arrivals: that things don't look good. She asks how she can help, not just medically but with comfort. She brings more coffee and a new plate of cookies. She answers questions and then slips quietly away.

My grandfather sleeps and sleeps and sleeps. We adjust his oxygen mask and his blankets. We tell him that we are there. We go back and forth about whether he needs his glasses—they rest so heavily on his nose, but without them, if he opens his eyes, will he be able to see anything? My mom sits by his bedside and rests her hand on his. Her voice trembles. She rises and hugs me with fierceness. We tell Grandpa again that we love him, and we wait again, and switch chairs again and then wait some more.

At one point his eyelids flutter.

"He's waking up!" Caroline alerts us and we all circle around in expectation. The bedside of a dying man is a thin place indeed.

We wait quietly motionless to see what wisdom he might impart, what last words he might have for us. He slowly and painfully opens his eyes and draws in ragged air, looking around at all of us standing there, holding our collective breath. Then he speaks.

"This is all *bullshit*," he says.

C'est la vie.

A group of hummingbirds is called a shimmer. These tiny, iridescent fliers are nature's smallest, ranging from two and a half to six inches, tip to tail. Their legs are so short that their feet serve only for grasping and balancing on perches. To move even an inch, they must use their wings. There are twenty-five species in North America, Black-chinned and Ruby-throated, Anna's and Allen's, Calliope and Broad-tailed and Violet-crowned and Buff-bellied, and the feistiest of them all, the Rufous.

When measured in body lengths, the Rufous Hummingbird travels one of the lengthiest migratory journeys of any bird on earth. Notes the Cornell Lab, "At just over 3 inches long, its roughly

3,900-mile movement (one-way) from Alaska to Mexico is equivalent to 78,470,000 body lengths."[5] Rufous Hummers are known for dive-bombing other visiting hummingbirds, songbirds that outweigh them by a significant amount, or even chipmunks that wander too close to their nests. They're scrappy and pugilistic because they have to be. It's that hard-bitten tenacity that carries them all the way from the southernmost parts of Mexico to Alaska's Alexander Archipelago.

While in Mexico they feast on the nectar that will carry them on their long journeys, a wonder of nature and instinct. They breed in the colder climes of the Pacific Northwest, up into Canada and Alaska and then, when the temperatures start to plummet, they turn around and do it all again, though not along the same paths. In spring they migrate along the western coastlands. In the fall, they travel south along the Rocky Mountains.

Migration is a marvel, yet it can also be a source of grief for the armchair ecologist. Ed Yong chronicled the disruption of the path of songbirds who flew into the huge blue beams of Manhattan's annual 9/11 memorial.

Tribute in Light, across seven nights of operation, waylaid about 1.1 million birds. The beams reach so high that even at altitudes of several miles, passing birds are drawn into them. Warblers and other small species congregate within the light at up to 150 times their normal density levels. They circle slowly, as if trapped in an incorporeal cage. They call frequently and intensely. They occasionally crash into nearby buildings.

Migrations are grueling affairs that push small birds to their physiological limit. Even a night-long detour can sap their energy reserves to fatal effect. So whenever 1,000 or more birds are caught within Tribute in Light, the bulbs are turned off for 20 minutes to let the birds regain their bearing. But that's just one source of light among many. . . . At other times, light pours out of sports stadiums and tourist attractions, oil rigs and office buildings. It pushes back the dark and pulls in migrating birds.[6]

Even we amateur ornithologists, tracking birds with notebooks or apps or just our memories, may notice dates shifting as migrations inch earlier and earlier. While for us the difference between, say, March 15 and March 18 is not even a handful of days—barely even registering—for a migrating bird, dependent on enough increased body weight for a long journey, that date creeping sooner can be catastrophic. At their extremes, migrating birds perch on the razor's edge of what is possible. One day's less nectar can send a hummingbird plummeting into the Gulf of Mexico. One glowing baseball diamond can waylay enough songbirds to begin the dominoes falling toward a population collapse.

A number of years ago, I joked on Twitter that I was considering getting into birding later on in life—"in twenty years or so," I quipped. Almost immediately a number of birders cautioned me that I shouldn't wait that long. That many of the birds I could see today might not be around in twenty years. Their chastening worked: my love of birds took flight soon thereafter. But I was unprepared for all the ways that becoming a birder is to be pulled regularly between sorrow and transcendence.

To fall in love with the world of birds—their habits and calls and colors and songs and patterns and behaviors and personalities—is to open one's heart to the anguish of losing so very, very much. But then, loving anything at all comes with a risk. And without love, who are we?

The parables of Scripture remain on the church's repeat playlist in part because they speak marvelously to even the youngest and newest among us. It takes a lot of explanation to make sense of Paul's circumcision passages in Galatians, but my three-year-old daughter understands that if someone is hurt, we shouldn't leave them on the side of the road, even if we are in a hurry. Parables grow with us—working on us and in us and through us in ways mere facts seldom do. A story, a really *good* story, becomes part of us. We carry it with us always.

Take the prodigal son. A man has two sons and the younger decides he's tired of waiting for his fortune. He wants it now. His father acquiesces, and the son takes off for a far country where he lives out the expected story: wild living, squandered wealth. At rock bottom he finds himself working a humiliating, degrading job, so racked with hunger that he considers digging into the food the pigs—utterly unclean in his culture—are eating.

Then, a light bulb moment.

Scripture describes it this way: *he came to himself.* This in-breaking of awareness is a hallmark of gospel transformation. A spark of understanding. A divine revelation. In the book of Acts literal scales fall from Saul's eyes. And then, repentance. Sin has a way of dulling the senses, but the holy tendrils of reality can begin to bring us back to ourselves.

I picture the son, his robes tattered, his face smudged with mud and worse, broken in body and spirit, experiencing this shimmering flutter of contrition, and looking up.

A group of hummingbirds is called a tune. With their buzzing wings and hoarse chirrups they are a miniature percussion section, delicate in the flick of their tongues, the way they alight on an impossibly thin branch that barely bends under their feather-weight. Two Allen's Hummingbirds nest in our backyard, the male with his shimmering orange throat, the female iridescent green. They visit the honeysuckle and the gladiolas and the blossoms on the nectarine trees.

At twilight, the lady hummingbird sits motionless in the towering shrub overhanging our yard's western edge. The male flits in and out through the foliage and it dawns on me that they must have a nest there, woven from grasses and no bigger than a teacup. My kingdom for hummingbird babies! I climb our children's swing set and sit at the top with binoculars, scanning the shrubs for any hint of one, but I see only green and shadow, green and shadow. Soon I realize I must look like a peeping Tom to our neighbors and I climb down.

My lack of success in spotting owls in the wild is on par with my inability to find nests. I'm terrible at spotting nests.

Down in Dana Point, right off the parking lot for Doheny Beach, sits a giant melaleuca tree filled with nesting Black-crowned Night Herons and Snowy Egrets. There is a six-foot-tall sign near the tree reminding beachgoers to leave the birds alone but also informing passersby to stop and take a gander at these magnificent creatures. On a recent visit I stood for a quarter-hour beneath the tree, gazing up with my binoculars, listening to a cacophony of squawks, com-pletely unable to find even a single nest.

"See any?" A couple of older gentlemen in polo shirts and Dockers wandered up to my elbow, squinting in the bright morning sun.

"I can *hear* them," I said, pivoting under the tree for a better angle.

"There's one," the second man said, lifting his cane to gesture. "And another. Lots of 'em up there. Just watch where you stand."

He lowered the cane and swept it over the pavement. I glanced down and noticed, for the first time, giant white piles of droppings, including one atop which I'd inadvertently planted my right foot.

Not only did I struggle to spot the giant nests of huge shorebirds next to a sign saying, "Yes, hi, there are giant shorebirds in this tree," but I'd missed the giant piles of their poop on the ground, too. Daryl says I read too much to possibly be this unobservant, but here we are. I'll find a typo in *The New York Times* without trying, but I'll also walk right into a massive pile of bird droppings while on the lookout for nests I can't locate even though I know they are *right there*. There's a parable here, to be sure.

I grew up in evangelical churches that leaned hard on the individual, personal aspects of sin. I knew from an early age that *it was my sin that held him there*. We were encouraged to live rightly, to search our consciences, to work hard to be good. Piety was paramount. My parents regularly taught my sisters and me to apologize to one another after a spat, to say we were sorry. To forgive.

This foundation was a good one, particularly for a child as earnest as I was, but it was not complete. Individual sin—guilt, culpability, the desperate wickedness of the human heart—can't really be overstated. Though we weren't Calvinists, we were sold on total depravity. Yet sin is deeper and wider and more woven into the fabric of cultures and kingdoms and societies and economies than what I, personally, choose to do. Systemic sin is real. Corporate sin is real. When we publicly confess our sins together in worship at my church we don't say, "Heavenly Father, I confess that *I* have sinned against you in thought, word, and deed." Instead we say *we*. *We* have sinned. *We* have not loved you with our whole heart. *We* have not loved our neighbor as ourselves. Each one of us is individually complicit, but we also participate in sin as a whole. It is nearly impossible to work or shop or invest or fill up our cars with gasoline without taking part in systems of evil. Theologian Karl Barth called them "lordless powers."

Environmental concerns bump up against these powers. We can't point a finger to Mr. Bad Guy who is responsible for the death of the last Northern White Rhinoceros. There is no one corporation or culture or person who singlehandedly pushed the Kirtland's Warbler to the edge of extinction. There are bad actors, certainly: companies seeking profit over sustainability, lobbyists and senators and representatives and ordinary people choosing wrong over environmental right. When the guy living across the lake from my parents learned it was illegal to clear-cut shoreline footage because of its devastating environmental effects, he did it anyway. When the Department of Natural Resources slapped him with a heavy fine and required him to replant the trees or face a steeper consequence, he paid it and then planted two-inch saplings that will take fifty years to grow as tall as the forest he destroyed.

It is my children who see baby pine trees across the lake when they visit Grandma and Grandpa's house, rather than the lush, old-growth forest. There will be fewer ducks and more chemical runoff into the lake because of his lawn. And yet not only the effects but the responsibility falls on us all. *We confess. We have sinned.*

Often it is only something as jarring as death that puts us face to face with sin and brokenness, unable to look away. In normal seasons we can be as slow to recognize it as I am with the nests of birds, even though the signs are everywhere. We blunder about, wondering just what it is that has gone wrong and how we might have stepped in so much guano without noticing. Calvinists speak of total depravity, the idea that basically *everything* has gone wrong, from our motives to our actions. Sin is pervasive, brokenness constantly at hand. But when it's the water we swim in, it can become particularly difficult to truly see. Death removes our bandanna blindfolds with the snap of a wrist.

There it is. No looking away.

How does a person repent of corporate evil? Is it possible to turn from ecological sin without becoming a joyless recycling bin monitor? Or do we simply keep crowing that it isn't our fault and pass the buck to the next generation? Dietrich Bonhoeffer is credited with saying, "The ultimate test of a moral society is the kind of world that it leaves to its children." It's a test we are not passing.

A group of hummingbirds is called a bouquet. My sisters are back with flowers from the grocery store. They arrange them in vases on the windowsill overlooking the forests beyond and below. The sky is still that opaque, flat, colorless gray that plagues the Midwest from November through late spring.

The doctors and nurses are in and out, as is a caseworker who needs to make a transit plan, "just in case." I know she's simply doing her job, that people do sometimes rally out of a near-death state and need someplace to go—insurance won't allow him to live for weeks in the hospital when he isn't being treated to cure any longer—but she's also adding a layer of confusion to everyone's anticipatory grief. Should we try to manage home hospice two days from now if Grandpa is still alive? Will he be? Is it wrong to hope he dies in the hospital, without having to suffer the discomfort and loneliness of an ambulance ride where he might very well pass on to glory while in transit—a particularly grim possibility?

We sit and stew. I don't weigh in—I'm the one who leaves tomorrow. It isn't my place to make these decisions. My sisters head out to run another quick errand. Mom and Dad and Grandma are gathered by the head of Grandpa's bed, conferring in low voices.

"I can't manage him at home," Grandma says.

"I know," says my dad.

I pull out my computer and open up my Good Friday sermon. In three days we will remember the death of Jesus, worshiping in a service that ends in darkness and silence and grief. Today, in Wisconsin, the sun is just beginning to set.

8

DELIGHT

WARBLERS

Sorrow prepares you for joy.

RUMI

IT IS GETTING IN TOUCH with our own mortality that first alerts many of us to the delight of birding. Feeling the shortness of years, the finitude of our lives, the limits of our strength or health or abilities begin to slow us down enough to pause in beauty, noticing the gifts present in common things.

In *Zen and the Art of Motorcycle Maintenance*, Robert Pirsig points out a red-winged blackbird to his son as they ride their bike toward the Dakotas.

"I've seen *lots* of those, Dad!"

"Oh!" I holler back. Then I nod. At age eleven you don't get very impressed with red-winged blackbirds.

You have to get older for that.[1]

Young children can spot the wonder in a blackbird, a hummingbird, a sparrow, but by the preteen years, most are jaded to the blessings of nature and are hungry instead for the splashy, flashy, instant gratification of screens and songwriters and school dances. Some souls stay tethered to the rhythms of field and forest through adolescence and young adulthood, but not many. Our appetites are shaped by our environments and experiences. During the early pandemic, our toddler daughter would squeal with excitement over the prospect of a nature hike while her older brothers rolled their eyes. They'd been to Disneyland; she never had.

As the wear of aging humbles us, birds once again become winged harbingers of hope, reminders of the gift and grace of creation. Beginning as a birder is a bit like moving to a foreign country and slowly picking up the language. Road signs that were gibberish to us at first now give direction. Snippets of conversation transform from mere noise into story. There is a new world layered upon the old. It's always been there, but we lacked a legend and a map and the interest necessary to learn how to see. Once we begin to see, delight is just a wingtip away.

"I can't believe how much I was smiling over a hawk," one friend told me. "I hadn't seen any hawks in the canyon for some time, and then, all of a sudden, there one was and I couldn't contain the joy."

A few years ago, in the weeks leading up to Ash Wednesday, I pondered adding a practice to my Lenten season rather than giving something up. In the past I'd set aside sugar or caffeine or television as a fast of sorts, giving up in order to lean into the passion of Christ and the holy work of the season. But with the pandemic still receding in the rearview mirror, an ascetic practice seemed unduly harsh. We'd given up so much for so long. My spirit felt so heavy.

As I pondered, I remembered my birding friend Paul Wallace's occasional puns. He'd head out into the forests near his Georgia home or sit in a marsh or wait on the outskirts of a parking lot and ask for a "bird from the Lord." I sent him a note: Would he mind if I borrowed his practice (and its liturgically whimsical phrase) and invited others to do the same? He was delighted.

Thus began the first annual #abirdfromthelord, a Lenten season where I committed to sit outdoors for ten minutes every day awaiting whatever birds God might send my way. The goal was to cultivate stillness, awareness, gratitude, and prayer. I invited my church into it and a couple of days later received a tongue-in-cheek text from my friend Clayton: *I went down to Dana Point Harbor and prayed for a bird from the Lord and then I saw a crow eating a Del Taco wrapper. What do you think that means?*

Presbyterian friends joined in, but so did Catholics and Lutherans, Episcopalians and spiritual-but-not-religious types. We hashtagged and shared photos. On Fridays, my sabbath where I generally stay offline, Paul led the exercise. As Lent wore on, the story was picked up by the *National Catholic Reporter*. A Jewish bird photographer who calls himself the Avian Rebbe joined our ranks. I sat quietly in our backyard, the local park, the church parking lot and waited, prayerfully. I saw juncos and pelicans, bushtits and robins, pigeons and crows, egrets and sandpipers. But what I hadn't planned on was that Lent often falls smack in the middle of the spring migration. In California, spring means *warblers*.

Warblers are neotropical migrants, with many species spending their winters in Latin America, the Caribbean, or even as far down as South America. In spring they head north, donning their finest breeding plumage in all its colorful glory. Warblers are the Easter eggs of the birding world, round, bright in color—yellow and green, blue and orange, cerulean, red, and chestnut—and difficult to spot. It isn't uncommon to stand beneath a tree buzzing with warblers yet struggle to see a single one. It becomes clear why a group of warblers is called a confusion. When I returned from a recent spring bird walk and complained of a sore spine, a friend told me that's called "warbler neck." Small and sharp-beaked and incredibly active, these insectivorous birds favor the highest leafy perches where they flit and hop and sing and snatch bugs right out of the air. My birding friend Paul has a whole photography series of slightly out of focus warblers behind leaves. (His explanation is that the warblers themselves are just inherently blurry. Paul is the best.)

Warblers fly hundreds or even thousands of miles each spring and fall. Some, like the Blackpoll Warbler, summer in Alaska and winter in northern Bolivia, a migratory distance of over seven thousand miles that includes a treacherous flight across the Gulf of Mexico. They come through our parks and forests and backyards but usually stay for only a brief period of time. Warbler migrations are why birders should be exempt from going to work during spring's peak week. Naturalist Mike Birgin notes, "For many North American birders, wood warblers represent everything exciting, compelling, and immediate about birding. . . . Their spring arrival in my part of the world represents one of the most joyous—but far too brief—spans in our birding calendar."[2]

Birds this stereotypically cute earn lots of nicknames. Yellow-rumped Warblers are "butterbutts," American Redstarts are "fire lanterns," and the whole stock of warblers are "avian jewels" or "tropical fish." Their return sends birdwatchers out into the forests and marshes in droves. I don't exaggerate when I say we wait all year for this. The fall migration is lovely in its own way, particularly because many regions get to see certain warblers for the only time all year due to different seasonal migratory patterns. But fall's migrators tend to sport muted hues and sing more subdued songs. Breeding time is over and they are all business on their way south.

In spring and fall, these tiny-feathered creatures, most weighing no more than a deck of cards, fill their bellies with insects and start their journeys. Most fly nocturnally, as do the majority of other migrating songbird species. This offers three advantages: first, it helps them avoid predators like hawks and falcons. Warblers are not especially gifted long-haul fliers and are easy prey for eagle-eyed raptors. Second, migratory flight creates a great deal of heat, and cooler evening air helps the birds regulate their core temperatures without expending extra energy. Finally, the air in the atmosphere is typically not as turbulent at night, allowing for easier, smoother flight paths.[3]

Resources like BirdCast track seasonal migration, reporting estimates of how many birds are in the air on any given day in various areas of the world. In the spring, waterfowl go first, ducks and geese and swans heading north as soon as lakes and marshes begin to thaw. Then come eagles and hawks, hardy native sparrows, Purple Martins, sapsuckers, kinglets. A few birds migrate quite early or quite late—sandpipers, for example, are divided into species that head north in late January and those that wait until late April or even May. Near the end of spring, birds more sensitive to fluctuating temperatures, those who have wintered in the tropics, wing northward: grosbeaks, thrushes, buntings, tanagers, vireos, orioles, and, of course, warblers.

Renowned birder Kenn Kaufman notes, "For many birders, warblers are particular favorites; there are several places in the country where you can see more than 30 species of these tiny, colorful gems during the course of the season."[4] Every spring, over a billion birds migrate over the state of California. At peak migration, there will be five hundred million birds in flight on a single evening across the nation. I fall asleep during spring nights picturing the thousands of warblers and flycatchers and sparrows and orioles and buntings and vireos winging their way north over my bed.

It beats counting sheep all to heck.

In his *Book of Delights*, poet Ross Gay tells of how he set out to experiment with the daily practice of writing a short essay about something that delighted him.

> It didn't take me long to learn that the discipline or practice of writing these essays occasioned a kind of delight radar. Or maybe it was more like the development of a delight muscle. Something that implies that the more you study delight, the more delight there is to study. . . . I felt my life to be more full of delight. Not without sorrow or fear or pain or loss. But more full of delight. I also learned this year that my delight grows—much like love and joy—when I share it.[5]

It is the loaves and fishes parable of abundance, that when we share that which nourishes us, there is not less to go around, but more. Delight invites more delight. Delight shared is multiplied exponentially, not pared down to less.

I grew up in a family suspicious of delight. Our German heritage plus our Protestant work ethic put us in a constant state of what Brené Brown calls dress-rehearsing for tragedy.[6] That and my father's profession as an insurance agent, where he waded through actuarial tables and wrote checks to people who'd crashed their Jet Skis through their piers, smashed up deer with their cars, or lit their homes on fire with unattended scented candles. He sometimes read us death statistics at the dinner table. I learned not to ask whether I could get a trampoline for my birthday (so dangerous!) or ride my boyfriend's snowmobile (even dangerouser!). One Saturday morning we began our yard work with my father handing me a shovel and cautioning, "Be careful. Do not hit your sister in the face with this."

We weren't joyless. We played sports and laughed at comedies and argued good-naturedly over board games on nights filled with what my sisters and I referred to as FFAs—Forced Family Activities. My father was the king of goofy-but-true tales where he ended up the punch line, and my mother's favorite storyteller was Jim Gaffigan. We were happier than most.

Yet delight is a step beyond. To delight is to trust in the spark of glee and felicity that transcends the sensibility of happiness. If happiness is a smile, delight is a bounce into the air, a thrill, a rush of cheerful rapture. Delight warrants a kind of self-forgetfulness that is purely in the moment. Transported. Transcendent.

When I wrote my book on happiness, a theological exploration of whimsy, most of my writing friends commented that it sounded fun or cheerful or interesting. But one, prone to bouts of deep depression, named it most accurately.

"That sounds excruciating," she told me.

Delving deeply into delight is impossible unless we are also in touch with sorrow. The warblers arrive only after arduous journeys across barren deserts and windswept seas. Delight requires risk and trust. It is a radical undertaking, not for the faint of heart.

When twenty-eight-year-old poet Denise Levertov sent a fan letter to the older, more established poet William Carlos Williams in 1951, he responded with wonderful self-deprecation:

> I am not what [my admirers] think. . . . They deserve something more. It is in fact the duty of the artist to assume greatness. I cannot. What a fool. Here I sit in my little hole like a toad. Thank you for your letter.[7]

This began a years-long writerly friendship, its correspondence now collected in Christopher MacGowan's *Letters of Denise Levertov and William Carlos Williams*. As they began to trust one another, slowly the delight between them grew. (Though Williams never stopped with the self-deprecation, which, really, is its own type of delight.)

The psalmist invites delight in the Lord, using the Hebrew word for "pleasure." As a child of the church, I often felt comfort from God. I've received assurance, forgiveness, challenge, and conviction. But I'd never really experienced delight. I'd read stories of ancient church mothers and fathers falling into fits of ecstasy, transported in rapturous love of their Creator, and I would think, "Good for them. They didn't have roller coasters or gourmet chocolate."

But then I began birding, and the ridiculous idea occurred to me that perhaps taking delight in the Lord was less about sitting still with an open Bible, trying to will myself into a joyful feeling, and more about drinking deeply of the delights God plants over every square inch of the world. I'd been attempting to force delight and all the while God was sending warblers past my window. As Williams wrote to Levertov, "You can't manufacture a mood out of whole cloth but when it comes you have to be ready for it."[8]

Most birders have a gentle, nerdy excitement over birds in general. Sure, nearly all of us have some lifers we really want to see (*my kingdom for a Spotted Owl!*). We may plan vacations around nature preserves and wetlands (rumor has it that British evangelist and author John Stott requested an extra day be added to all his speaking engagements so he could go birding). But also: we just *like* birds, period. Birders sit willfully—joyfully!—motionless in buggy forests for hours to catch the wing-whisper of a rare Kirtland's Warbler, but are also pretty jazzed about a pigeon dive-bombing a pizza crust in a subway tunnel. Birders have a childlike enjoyment of the avian world that can be downright infectious. It can also be outright baffling to those who don't share it.

On an episode of *This American Life*, Noah Strycker told Ira Glass the story of bringing visitors to the penguin colonies he was studying in Antarctica:

> They go into their colony, they see the baby penguins, which are super cute. And then, like, day five or so, people get up in the morning and they're like, where are we going to go today? And you say, we're going to a penguin colony. And there's this look that I've learned to recognize. It's like, I've just been to eight other penguin colonies in the past four days. How is this one going to be any different? But for me, I have never felt that look in my whole life. I have never got penguined out.[9]

Either you get the birding obsession or you don't, and if you don't, there's no need to fret. Aging has a way of slowing many of us down enough that we finally begin to look up.

Still, if you aren't there yet, the passion of birders may strike you as odd at best. We truly never get penguined out. When I first developed a birding passion, Daryl would lay down ground rules for our date nights.

"You get to tell me two bird facts," he'd tell me. "Just two, and you will have my full attention for both, and then please can we talk about something else?"

He's coming around, though. I recently caught him downloading the Merlin app. It's only a matter of time before he gets a khaki vest. I remain optimistic because that's what birders do. It's who we are. In fact, even the way birders search for their quarry tends to breed optimism. The simple physical act of looking up has proven psychological benefits. Being outdoors has been shown by hundreds of studies to improve one's mood. Plus, birding takes us deeper into the natural world. We begin to notice that the same old window box or backyard or hiking trail is actually subtly different from day to day as the seasons turn and the weather changes.

To bird is to be attentive to the gift of delight.

I've witnessed the end-of-life dance more times than I can count, and there's a knack to keeping the circles of grief properly ordered. Of course, there are layers and exceptions, but in general losing a spouse or a child are the cruelest blows. As a hospice chaplain I was trained to attend first to the patient and then to those touched most immediately and profoundly by the impending loss—the husband or the wife or the parents. When the person dying is older, we look first to their spouse, if they have one, and then to their children. After that, grandchildren. I watch as my family intuitively orders these circles, giving Grandma space and time, ushering Uncle John into the best seat when he arrives and she takes a break, tending to my mother and making sure she eats, all while making sure Grandpa is never alone.

My sister Caroline sings. My sister Caitlyn smooths his brow. Everyone keeps bringing food and now we have mountains of fruit and quinoa and chips and candy and organic Alaskan salmon and gluten-free crackers because everyone has their own dietary thing but also, everyone wants to share because food is love, and one of the only things we have left to do is to feed one another and wait.

We ask if we can smuggle my sister's dog in from her car. The answer is no, but Nurse Beth does try her darnedest to get it approved. I don't think it is too much of a stretch to say that my grandfather loved animals more than people. It wasn't that he didn't love people. He did. It's just that he didn't like them very much. He *loved* animals. Not only his cats—always shelter cats—and dogs—German Shepherds and Black Labrador Retrievers—but the birds and turtles and every deer that meandered through his backyard. He never had much to say when I called, but if I asked about the animals, he would talk for a while. Despite his grouchiness, animals were always a backdoor into delight.

We mention to Beth that Grandpa is enjoying the little bit of water we're offering him when we moisten his lips with the medical sponges.

"It's okay for him to have that, right?" I ask.

"He can have Sprite, if he wants," she jokes.

"Actually, he's diabetic but loves sugar," I say. "That wouldn't matter anymore, would it? I mean, we could give him Sprite?"

"Absolutely!" She says. I turn to the room.

"Did he like Sprite?" All I remember is that he liked Heileman's Old Style and gin, but I doubt the nurse's station is stocked with either.

"Pepsi!" My dad pipes up. My parents have been bringing Grandma and Grandpa Sunday lunches—Subway sandwiches and diet sodas—Grandpa's belly full but his sweet tooth unsated for years.

"We have Coke, is that okay?" Beth asks.

"Of course," we say, but she notices our tiny hesitation and moments later I stumble upon her walking out of the elevator with a Pepsi I'm certain she purchased out of her own pocket.

"We had to bring him his favorite," she says.

Caroline sponges the inside of his mouth with just a few drops and a flush of delight comes across Grandpa's face. He closes his lips around the sponge and then opens them again, and she refills it and offers him the sugary liquid again and again. Everyone's face is wet, struck by the gift we've been given, to witness one more instance of delight.

9

GRIEF

ALBATROSSES

The poet is like this prince of the clouds,
who haunts the storm and mocks the archer;
but exiled on earth surrounded by jeers,
his giant wings make him helpless to walk.

CHARLES BAUDELAIRE

W E DON'T ALWAYS RECOGNIZE LAST moments. People die in accidents, natural disasters, acts of violence. Life is unpredictable, and death, like birth, comes at its own pace.

Yet as I press a hand to my grandfather's forehead, I know this is the last time I will see him alive on this earth. It's Wednesday morning. Grandma and I drove back to the hospital today after our Maxwell House and cocoa and found Grandpa further along the path. We take our moments with him.

My aunt and uncle spent last night in hospital-issued recliners that look comfortable but aren't. As they begin to gather their things to go back to Grandma's for a shower, Nurse Beth stops them.

"You might want to stay," she says.

The whole family is gathered. My parents came back earlier this morning. My grandmother and I arrived at eight. An hour later, my sisters and cousins walked in. We are all here now, sitting and standing around the room, spilling into the hallway.

Grandpa has entered the active stages of dying. His skin is cooling, his breath slowing, his hands and feet are beginning to mottle. He is dying, and I need to leave for the airport by 11 a.m. It's 10:42.

Everyone hangs back to give me a few final moments, continuing the respectful dance of *your turn, my turn* we've all been doing for the past twenty-four hours. In a decade and a half of ministry, I've seen it all at hospital bedsides. Transcendence and grace, forgiveness and mercy. But unbelievably heinous behavior, too: tantrums and shouting and cousins making threats. I once watched a woman storm into an ICU waving her boyfriend's last will and testament as a doctor pumped violent CPR onto his crackling chest.

"It all goes to me!" she yelled. "Everything he has is mine!"

Death brings out the best and worst in people, and I'm proud of how our little cadre has managed. It's never clear how a family will navigate a loss of such magnitude until they're in it. None of this is easy, but grace and kindness are evident across the board, a balm for us all.

I put a hand on Grandpa's forehead and am suddenly at a loss for words. I notice the strength of his arms—the muscled biceps of a much younger man. My breath catches. I want to say everything, to somehow make it all better, or at least to offer some final comfort or grace. I'm a little bit ashamed at the notion that such a thing would even be possible, and if it was, that I would be the one person in this sea of suffering who could solve it. That, too, is part of the grief: we all want to help, to save everyone in this room from the anguish that is to come, but there is nothing more anyone can do. Being present in pain is all we have.

Grandpa may be beyond hearing, or he might be acutely aware of every shifting molecule of this world as he reaches for the next one. I feel desperate to stay longer and desperate to leave, to drive south and away from the grief that threatens to press all the air out of my lungs.

"Grandpa, it's Courtney," I say. "I just wanted to say . . . I wanted to say that I love you so much. Thank you for everything."

Our years of moments flash past—his fishing boat, his bird feeders, the stiff cotton of his jeans, his smile, his newspaper held open as he sat in front of the picture window, his short, high laugh, the blue of his eyes, the red bandanna folded and sticking out of his back pocket, the wheelchair he used in recent years, after the diabetes forced an amputation. I remember the stacks and stacks of trade paperbacks and library books, of how Grandpa only liked to read men, but he flipped through my books, too. I remember the curve of his shoulders as he bent over his basement tool bench or his green tackle box. I remember the deep creases etched in the back of his neck by years of sun. I remember how he greeted me each time with, "Hiya, Court." And then there is the aching, awful realization that the body before me in its hospital gown is about to return to the dust.

There is nothing more to say, and I am standing in a hospital room surrounded by sisters and parents and cousins and my grand-father's wife of sixty-four years and his only daughter and his only son. There is not much time left, barely any, and it's time for me to go.

"Thank you," I say again. "I love you. I love you forever."

I stroke his forehead one more time and then step back and away, devouring every detail: the white sheets, the flowers on the windowsill, the balloons tied to the cabinet handle, the pictures my children colored to brighten his room, Grandpa's gray-blonde hair and strong arms and long fingers. I want to remember the entirety of this moment, but I also want to forget it completely so I can picture him as he was when I was in pigtails, when he smelled of Swisher Sweets and piney air and Heileman's and fish from the lake and charcoal from the grill.

"I love you," I say once more.

And then I'm driving south.

Grief unmoors us. It throws us off balance. It crumbles away what we once thought was certain. It can push us to the edge of who we are until we topple over into the chasm beyond. In high school one of my youth group leaders experienced a death in his family, one that followed too soon after many others. He got into his truck and drove away and we didn't know where he was for days. He never told us.

In grief we require tenderness and time, but we live in a world of brutality and hurry. The average workplace allows just three days off for the death of a spouse, and even fewer for the death of a parent, sibling, or child. We are asked to move on before we've even begun to realize the number of ways our lives have been shattered. How can we begin to pick up the pieces before we have discovered all that's broken?

I once heard a cancer survivor speak of witnessing a stranger break down in the produce aisle of a supermarket. The stranger stood amid the tomatoes and onions and avocados with her hands at her sides and simply *sobbed*. The cancer survivor thought this was odd and planned to keep her distance until she noticed the woman's bald head peeking out from under a scarf.

"Oh," she realized. "She's one of *us*."

She went over to the woman and wrapped her arms around her, whispering, "I know. I'm so, so sorry. It's so hard. I know."

She held her there in the store for half an hour while other shoppers gave them a wide berth.

"I never learned her name," she told me. "But in those moments, she needed to be held."

How would our lives change if we approached one another with this same gentleness? How might we be transformed if we could meet one another in grief with the compassion Jesus shows when he stands vigil at Lazarus's tomb? He does not move quickly to reminders that all will be well, that they needn't be sad, that Lazarus is moments away from reappearing, and anyway, one day we will all rejoice at the wedding supper of the Lamb. Instead, he weeps.

Yes, friends, he says with his tears, *the grief is profound. The loss is deep. The pain is real.*

Do not rush it.

Humans aren't the only animals who grieve. Dogs grieve. Cats grieve. Killer whales have been spotted pushing their dead calves around for days.[1] Elephants and apes mourn. Birds do, too.

Take the albatross. We don't see many of these in Southern California, though occasionally a Northern Pacific one will end up near Catalina or Coronado Island. They spend most of their lives far out at sea, hunting for prey over thousands of miles. Besides the weeks they spend nesting, they are completely pelagic. When local birders manage to spot one that's wandered close to our shores—birds of this kind are known, delightfully, as vagrants—the message boards go bananas.

Albatrosses commonly go months without touching land. They have been clocked flying at nearly eighty miles per hour. They stay aloft using dynamic soaring, a roller coaster technique that makes use of slower wind speeds at ocean level and higher ones above it to climb up and down without expending precious energy to flap their wings. Albatrosses fly as far as a thousand miles on a single outing.[2] They return to nesting atolls no bigger than aircraft carriers after exploring thousands of miles of empty ocean. They're known to predict the weather,[3] which is good because they exist in some of the most uninhabitable regions of the planet.

Most albatrosses spend the majority of their lives at the three latitudes just above Antarctica, known to mariners as the Roaring Forties, Furious Fifties, and Screaming Sixties. At these latitudes, regular winds blow across the open ocean at thirty miles per hour, and stormy ones up to a hundred and fifty. That's category four hurricane speed, for anyone keeping track. Or, as an albatross might put it, delightful weather.

At age eight or nine the Laysan Albatross mates for life, after a lengthy courtship. Each pair lays only one egg per year, and raising their single chick to become self-sufficient can take up to nine months. If an albatross chick dies, its parents will wait until the following year before mating again. If the male or female of a mated pair dies, the other will mourn for years, ignoring all possible new partners until they are ready to court again.[4] Some never will be.

Albatrosses commonly live fifty years or more. In fact, the oldest known bird currently on earth is an albatross, a female named Wisdom who hatched in 1951 on Midway Atoll and is still, at time of this chapter's writing, alive (and laying eggs!) at seventy-one years of age.

With the largest wingspan of any living bird—over eleven feet—albatrosses are regal, powerful, and majestic both in the air and on the water. Ancient sailors revered them. Their name comes from the Arabic word for "diver," their order—*Procellariformes*—from the Latin for "violent storm." Because they spend much of their lives so far out at sea—most nesting only on remote islands—scientists still have much to learn about them. There is a decent amount of disagreement over even the basics. There are between thirteen and twenty-four species worldwide, either two or three or four genera, possibly more, maybe fewer. There's an air of mystery around albatrosses, and I like to think they prefer it that way. Not every species wants to be a house finch.

The albatross is best known in modern mythology as a curse of sorts. An "albatross around the neck" means an awkward and shameful burden. The idea comes from Samuel Coleridge's 1798 epic poem "The Rime of the Ancient Mariner," where an albatross, then seen as a sign of good luck for sailors, is shot by the mariner with a crossbow, an act of violence that is immediately followed by a series of mishaps for the entire crew. The other sailors, angry with the mariner for his misdeed and their resulting misfortune, tie the dead albatross around his neck as a sign of his guilt.

An albatross around the neck is not an inapt metaphor for grief. A massive, deceased seabird, awkward and ungainly and gruesome and beautiful, bouncing against a person's chest would make simple daily tasks arduous in the extreme. Sometimes I wish grief was as visible as an albatross necklace. It'd make us kinder, I think. Or at least remind us to give one another space.

People tend to die how they lived. Pleasant folks are pleasant up until the end, unpleasant ones unpleasant. Not only that, but family systems don't suddenly become healthier, kinder, or more logical amid anticipatory grief. Often, at the moment of death, anger or frustration that's been bottled up erupts, sometimes violently. Back during our chaplaincy training, Daryl's pager went off in the wee hours of the night and he sprang from our bed and threw on dress clothes. When he arrived on a medical floor of the hospital we served, a security guard asked him to remove his tie and name tag.

"They can choke you with one and stab you with the other," he said. "I've called for backup, but right now it's just you and me."

No one teaches you about this kind of thing in seminary.

Daryl followed the guard to a room filled with a hulking, raging family apoplectic with grief at the death of their patriarch. The guard motioned for Daryl to follow him as he put his body between the family and a tiny, trembling nurse. By the time Daryl came back to the on-call room to curl up with me hours later, he was wild-eyed.

"You okay?" I asked, rolling over, half asleep.

"Do I have a story," he said.

He never did find his tie.

The moment of death often shakes loose all that has been contained—the emotions, the tears, the words. No one sleeps very well with a loved one nearing the end of life, so fatigue that's been building for days or weeks hits like a tidal wave. Those who have held vigil at a bedside can develop health problems of their own, either because of the stress or because their own health issues were pushed aside out of necessity during the crisis. People tend to look at the death of a loved one as a finish line of sorts, and it is—for the loved one. But for those who remain, it is only the first step in a marathon of grief. Some cannot bear it. It isn't uncommon for weathered spouses to follow their partners in death before long.

It is actually possible to die of a broken heart.

Every person is grieving. Every person in our pews. Every person on our highways, in our supermarkets, at our offices and schools. Each person on your street, in your home. We will each experience seasons of more acute grief—the death of a loved one, the loss of a job or a dream, a natural disaster or house fire or health crisis— but we walk through small, simmering, chronic griefs every single day. It is the water we swim in, the air we breathe. To live is to experience loss. To love is to experience it all the more.

Yet many of us add guilt to our grief. We shove it down or away, telling ourselves we should be fine, should move on. Parishioners regularly shed tears with me about the death of a cat or dog and then apologize.

"I know it's just a pet," they'll say. Yet pets weave their way into the fabric of our families. Poet Scott Cairns began his short book *The End of Suffering* with a reflection on burying his dogs:

> The graves of two dogs may seem to some to be a relatively poor starting point—maybe even, to some, an insulting starting point—for this sort of inquiry. I hope not. I would never mean to equate the loss of a dog—or even the loss of two very good dogs—with every other occasion of human suffering. Still, I will not discount how hard, how sharp, even this loss remains, and how puzzling. It's the puzzlement, frankly, that makes even this current, specific grief remind me more generally of other grief, of other painful occasions, and of our overall predicament.
>
> In any case, as I shovel and as I weep over my big, sweet dogs, I wince off and on, a little embarrassed that in a world where each newscast and newspaper brings new images of

heart-wrenching human tragedy, I continue to be so broken up over losing my dogs.

My only defense for the moment will have to be that these really were extraordinarily good dogs.[5]

We need not weigh our grief on a cosmic scale, comparing it with the sadness of others or minimizing it in light of the world's many sufferings. Instead, we are invited to feel it. To sit with it. To notice and wrestle and befriend it. To set it aside and pick it back up again. There are shared patterns, but ultimately grief is individual. Each person must journey through their own. There is no reason to interrogate our tears. As Madeleine L'Engle notes, "Men wept freely before too much 'civilization' taught them that tears were unmanly."[6] I have sought to curtail my own tears because they risk looking unprofessional or—a particularly feminine fear—hysterical. A quick tear slipping down the cheek is dignified; a flood of them unsettles people.

Yet grief will not be tamed. We can shirk it but be certain it will come out in other ways—anger, bitterness, depression, an all-out nervous breakdown—or we can expose it to light and air, being patient with ourselves all the while. Grieving takes the time that it takes. It doesn't like to be hurried. For those of us prone to rushing, the achievers or speedsters or restless types, this is a hard lesson.

The only way out is through, and through will take time.

Some albatross species circumnavigate the globe at the stormiest latitudes on earth. They give me courage. Albatrosses prefer a stiff wind—easier for taking off—to sunny, calm days, and they are indefatigable in obtaining food for their chicks. The long incubation process for an albatross egg—seventy to eighty days—and the even

longer maturation process of an albatross from chick to fledgling—
up to a year—is one reason the pairs have such a lengthy courtship.
Females must be certain their male counterparts can help bring in
large amounts of food and nesting materials, as both partners
share in the incubation and raising of their young. Once chicks can
thermoregulate long enough to be left alone, both parents will head
out on foraging trips, doubling their chances of obtaining enough
food for their growing youngster.

In the avian world, albatrosses are outliers in size, weight,
lifespan, and maturation speed. Everything is bigger and takes
longer with an albatross. Because of their unique, windswept island
locations, studying albatrosses is a dangerous business. One scientist survived a near-shipwreck only to be marooned for five
months on Marion Island in the South Indian Ocean waiting for
rescue. He'd expected to visit this albatross nesting spot for just two
days[7]—but then he knew what he might be getting into. With great
birds comes great adventure. Not always fun, but big.

Famous for its World War II battle, Midway Atoll, a set of two tiny
islets totaling two and a half square miles in the Pacific Ocean, is
home to two million nesting albatrosses. That's an albatross every
two feet. Picture them: mostly Laysan, but some Black-footed and
the occasional Short-tailed as well. Glory. Guano. Gooney birds as
far as the eye can see.

The birds that nest on Midway have no natural predators—there
are monk seals around, but they're only looking for fish. Of course,
the waters of the Pacific hold sharks and orcas, but an albatross is
too lofty to become a snack for either. Occasionally Japan experiences a major earthquake, and the resulting tsunami can swamp

much of the atoll under nearly five feet of water. (This last happened in 2011, and over a hundred thousand nestlings drowned.[8])

The most consistent threat to albatrosses is human. Plastic trash from the Pacific garbage patch floods the atoll at a rate of a hundred pounds a day, and nesting albatrosses, eagerly seeking nourishment for their young, snap up bits that look like food. Albatross chicks lack the throat muscles necessary for regurgitation until they are at least four months old, so before then rates of sickness and death from ingesting plastic are high. One naturalist estimated that the average Midway albatross has over 50 percent of its intestinal tract filled with plastic.[9] Matt Brown, a guide from the US Fish and Wildlife service, noted, "Every single albatross in this landscape has been fed plastic."[10] Every single one.

And there it is again—the wonder and the grief, the holy awe at an incredible creature mixing with the sin that soaks its stain into the very bones of the earth. We have done this to the albatrosses with our cheap, imported toys, our beach sandals and disposable lighters and soda bottles. I think of Rachel Carson's reminder that "in nature, nothing exists alone."[11] I think of how many plastic Legos sit in plastic bins on plastic shelves in my own home. I think of mother and father birds seeking to nourish their babies and unknowingly feeding them poison instead.

Jesus asks, *Which of you, if your child asks for bread, will give him a stone?*

I look into trips to Midway, to see the beauty and carnage for myself, imagining for a second that we have thousands of dollars to throw toward my love of albatrosses. But I learn the area is closed to tourists, open only to government workers and naturalists. Also, I suspect I'd have daily panic attacks knowing the nearest solid ground tall enough to save me from a rogue wave was thousands of miles away.

There's grief there, too, in knowing there are birds I'll never encounter, in parts of the world closed to all but a select few. But then, fewer tourists is undoubtedly better for the albatrosses, and knowing they're sheltered in this way, at least for now, gives me a glimmer of hope.

On my drive south from Grandpa's hospital bed to the airport, I ask God for a place to stop and breathe, just for a moment. I pull off on a street labeled Swamp Lake Road—an unpromising name if ever there was one. A quarter-mile down the narrow road is a narrow bridge over a narrow lake. I park, bundle up, and wait for a break in the drizzling rain. I pray for a bird from the Lord.

As soon as I crack the car door I am greeted by a symphony. *Song Sparrows*. The woods are filled with my favorite birds, and as I watch, one hops out on the limb of a downed tree and scoots all the way out over the water, lifting its little face to the sky and opening its beak wide to join the chorus.

Even in grief, there is new hope, for the dead grieve no more. The work of grief is left to the living. The tears turn cold on my cheeks as I listen to the sparrows.

Goodbye, Grandpa, I whisper.

An hour later, I am in line at the airport when my father texts me. He is gone.

10

PARTNERSHIP

WRENS

Friendship is born at that moment
when one person says to another:
"What! You too? I thought that no one but myself . . . "

C. S. Lewis

ON THE WAY HOME, I walk through my connecting airport feeling far away, like I'm looking at everyone through the wrong end of a pair of binoculars. I purchase comfort food at a kiosk—Peanut M&Ms and a Diet Dr Pepper—and the clerk has to ask me three times for payment. Everything is distant and hushed. The world has sped up around me, but I feel submerged underwater. On the first plane, I toy with the magazine's crossword, fiddle with my Good Friday sermon, rest my eyes and open them again. On the second I try to sleep, but sleep won't come. We finally set our wheels down on a California runway, and soon I'm loading my bags into the trunk of our car in a dimly lit parking garage.

Landed, I text Daryl.

Waiting with hugs, he responds. *Plus, someone sent you vodka.*

I'm halfway home before I remember to take off my mask. Daryl meets me at the door, and I drop my bags and snuggle into his chest.

"I should wash my hands," I tell him.

"In a minute," he says. I lean in and inhale the scents of home.

An hour later, I'm brushing my teeth when Lincoln wakes up and bounds, smiling, into the bathroom. He puts a hand on my shoulder, a new habit he's picked up, a sort of *just between us adults* body language that is both charming and a little silly coming from a kid who isn't even tall enough for all the roller coasters yet. He asks how Great-Grandpa is doing. The last Lincoln heard, we still had months to prepare for what was to come.

I spit out my toothpaste and turn to face him.

"I'm so sorry, buddy," I say, "but Great-Grandpa died today."

He crumples in for a hug.

"I thought he was going to live two more months," he whispers.

"That was what the doctors thought, too," I said. "He died sooner than they thought, and very peacefully. I told him all about you. I told him that you loved him, and we hung up the pictures you all drew for him in his hospital room. Those were one of the last things he saw."

His wide blue eyes are wet. Mine are, too.

"That's good," he said. "And really sad."

"It is," I say. "Both things. I love you. I'm so glad to see you."

He turns to go.

In the morning we tell the younger two. Felicity briefly pauses in her play, sensing that this is a somber moment, but then she's off to her dress-up bin and breakfast and a mermaid puzzle. Wilson bursts into tears. He is our most tenacious child, and our

most tender. Later that night, as I tuck him into bed, the tears
come again.

"I didn't even *know* him!" he cries. "I didn't know anything
about him!"

I rub his back amid the fortress of pillows and stuffed animals
he meticulously constructs every night.

"Would it help if I told you about him?" I ask. He sniffles. Nods.

"Great-Grandpa had blonde hair and blue eyes, just like you," I
say. "He loved to build and fix things, just like you. He loved animals and taking care of them. He loved cats and dogs and birds,
especially. The only animals he really didn't like were squirrels."

Wilson's face pops up above a stuffed dragon.

"Really? Not squirrels?" he asks.

"Nope, he hated those squirrels. They always stole his birdseed."

Wilson chuckles.

"He liked to read books and watch westerns."

"What's a western?"

"A cowboy movie," I said.

"That sounds cool."

"He liked to be alone a lot," I said. "Sometimes he could be
pretty cranky."

Another chuckle.

"He cooked really good chicken on his grill. That's what I remember eating at his house most often. Grilled chicken and
baked potatoes."

The tears are streaming down Wilson's face now, and mine.

"I think I would have liked his chicken," he says.

"I think so, too," I say.

"I think I would have liked him," he says. I kiss his blonde baby
curls, already beginning to loosen with age.

"I know he would have loved you," I say.

It rains the day after I arrive home, a rare occurrence in our desert climate. I hike up into the hills, watching them explode with bird joy.

Did you hear? Did you see? It rained!

I pause for a moment in the middle of the trail and a Bewick's Wren hops from the thicket onto a branch at eye level, its tail a jaunty exclamation mark. It pauses to eye me curiously for a second and then tilts its head and opens its sharp beak in song. Bewick's Wrens are loud little things. Adults only grow to five inches long and weigh less than half an ounce, but *my* can they sing. Plus, their name is pronounced "Buick's," which is its own type of delight.

Wrens are mostly insectivorous. If you're lucky enough to have a pair of House Wrens nesting nearby, you'll experience a decline in flies, mosquitoes, and other buggy pests. While the largest wrens eat frogs and lizards, and nearly all occasionally eat fruit or seeds, most of their diet is entomological, making them welcome backyard guests.

Aristotle called the wren the king of birds, not for its size but for its ability to be "difficult of capture" and at war with the eagle.[1] Like many early animal fables, this isn't very factual, but I love to imagine tiny wrens—most no bigger than a coffee mug—wearing golden crowns, enthroned above eagles and osprey. Indeed, though most are brownish or grayish—many a birding book even goes so far as to call them "drab"—a few do sport ruby or golden feathers at their crowns.

Wrens sing complex and melodic songs. Songbirds possess a unique avian voice box called a syrinx. The syrinx houses two membranes similar to our vocal cords, but surrounded by muscles that are much more fine-tuned and sophisticated. Some species can vibrate either membrane independently, allowing them to sing two separate pitches simultaneously, one lower and one higher, essentially harmonizing with themselves.

Their volume is disproportionate to their diminutive sizes. They could perch easily on a pinkie finger, but they sound like electric flutes played through six-foot amps. Wrens like to hang out on the far tips of branches, bobbing gaily over trails or streams, singing their little wren hearts out. The Winter Wren sings up to thirty-six notes per second—many more than the human brain can comprehend. The Bewick's Wren starts hesitantly, a diva's throat-clearing, before launching into its arias. Tiny, curious, brown and gray, wrens would be the mice of the bird world, if mice trained with Maria Callas.

And then there is their antiphonal singing. Wrens make a joyful noise on their own, but in a duet the effect is transcendent. Some wrens sing together in pairs, weaving their voices into songs so intricate the human ear cannot separate one singer from another. Jennifer Ackerman notes in *The Genius of Birds*, "Plain-tailed wrens . . . sing rapidly alternating syllables so perfectly coordinated that it sounds like a single bird singing alone." When birds that typically sing together raise their voices alone "they leave longer gaps between song syllables, in which their partner normally interjects a brief note."[2] Like the three-legged race of a life-giving relationship, singing "with such high coordination requires being closely 'tuned-in' to your mate—and thus may communicate the strength of the pair, their bond and level of commitment to each other."[3]

When I think about friendship, I think about wrens. The interweaving of one melody with another, both made stronger, more intricate, and more beautiful in the process. Wrens' songs are richer in relationship. Ours are, too.

But here's the thing: American adults have lost the art of friendship. And the trajectory doesn't point toward things getting better any time soon. According to the American Survey Center, in 1990, 27 percent of adults said they had three or fewer close friends. In 2021 that number grew to 49 percent. In 1990, 3 percent of adults reported having no close friends. In 2021, that number grew to 12 percent.[4] Getting together is tricky for multiple reasons—chief among them simply being that most adults are exhausted most of the time—but it isn't just logistics or exhaustion holding us back. The problem runs deeper than that.

We've lost both sides of the duet because we are afraid. Afraid of knowing and being known. Afraid of singing our life's song in the presence of another and having that person respond with scorn or—worse—indifference. And now that we've lost the duet, we've begun to forget that such a beautiful, transcendent thing is even possible in the first place. It's an unconscious tragedy.

We're also, many of us, so filled up with the easy, low-stakes in-teractions of social media that we have begun to lose touch with our hunger for depth and intimacy in friendship. Digital interac-tions are candy. Quick, tasty, but ultimately not nourishing enough on their own. We can get by on a steady diet of likes and pings and shares for quite a while before we starve. But then, scurvy takes some time to develop, too.

I've been shocked—perhaps it's shocking that I was shocked, since it seems so obvious in retrospect—that in seasons when I log off social media for a time, within days I grow hungry for deeper connections of friendship. This isn't to decry relationships that are formed and fostered in digital spaces—I've met some of my dearest friends online—but it is a reminder that it is a tool to be used, one that will not hesitate to transform our appetites and ultimately consume us if left unchecked.

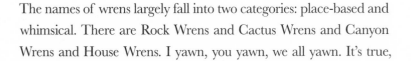

Early in ministry, a mentor pulled me aside and held up a stern finger.

"Don't isolate," he said. "You're young and capable and it will be very easy to go it alone. Until it isn't."

I ignored his advice for years. I had Daryl, after all, and a couple friends from college with whom I'd stayed loosely connected. Besides that, the people-facing elements of my vocation—committee meetings and corporate worship and conversations with congregants—seemed to be all the socializing my introvert's soul could absorb.

"I'm not a homebody," I told Daryl once. "I'm an alonebody."

I have always felt slightly guilty about this introversion. It seemed to be a defect of sorts, one that warranted a small apology, like not enjoying sushi or forgetting to bring the trashcans in from the curb on time. It didn't make me a bad person, but I could definitely try a little harder to be a better one. I was certain Jesus himself would never tire of small talk. But the more time I spend in the Gospels, the more I notice how frequently he retreated from the crowds. There he goes, up on a mountain. There he goes again, retreating to a garden. There he goes once more, slipping away through the throngs in Jerusalem. It was Jesus who told us to pray in our closets, alone. Take that, extroverts.

But still, I could sense that my song was anemic. We all need more voices in the choir than just our own.

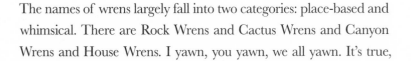

The names of wrens largely fall into two categories: place-based and whimsical. There are Rock Wrens and Cactus Wrens and Canyon Wrens and House Wrens. I yawn, you yawn, we all yawn. It's true, wrens aren't much to look at. The birding guide *Warblers* calls them "dumpy-bodied"—rude!—and many species are so shy and small they are far more likely to be heard than seen. Naming a wren after a geographical landmark feels like calling the Empire State Building "that tall thing on West 34th Street." Wrens deserve better—and some of them lucked out. There's the Musician's Wren, the Song Wren, the Flutist Wren, the Fairy Wren. There's even a species found in Western Mexico called the Happy Wren, its name another reminder of why God invites us into friendship: because at its depths, there is joy.

A handful of years back, fighting against both the sleep deprivation of young parenthood and time zone differences that can make telephone communication tricky, a couple of dear friends and I began using a video chat app instead. They'd send a message—five or ten or fifteen minutes about their day and their vocation and their family, challenges and triumphs and ordinary musings—and then I'd respond. They would sing, metaphorically speaking, and I'd sing back. These daily melodies have carried us through Covid uncertainty, political upheaval, interpersonal conflict, deaths in the family, life-altering choices, and the grindiness of the daily grind. We share highs, lows, and everything in between. They sing. I sing.

While we visit one another in person as often as we are able, the responsibilities of vocation and parenting mean these trips are few and far between. I am grateful for the gift of the daily songs that make up the bulk of our friendship's rhythm. These daily conversations are our modern equivalent of Jane Austen's letters, of telegrams in early Americana, of neighborly chats over the back fence. Words alone can't save us, but friendship certainly has a hand in placing our feet upon the rock.

These shared conversations have made me a better friend. A better listener. They are teaching me to be a weaver of song.

Back in California, after my whirlwind trip east to Grandpa's deathbed, I try to snap back into normal life, but I've forgotten how grief feels like a bruise. I cry when someone honks at me at a stoplight. I am in tears at texted memes, a postcard in the mail, the weather report. A friend sends over a flower arrangement. Another mails me a soft blue blanket. A third Door Dashes me a giant bottle of vodka while I am still on the plane home, which brings tears and also laughter. (At *most* I'm a three-drinks-a-week person. This bottle will last all year.)

My friend Anna and I carry one another through Holy Week, she leading her church in Massachusetts, me pastoring here in California. We talk each other through the preparation and listen to one another's tales of triumph and disaster big and small.

"Anna told me to be very gentle with myself," I tell Daryl.

"That's good advice," he says.

Anna and I don't give each other advice. Not really. We have an unspoken covenant not to start sentences with "At least . . ." or "If I were you . . ." unless we're explicitly asked to weigh in with our suggestions. But there is no way to take off the pastor hat entirely, and her ministry prowess inevitably bleeds over into our chats. I am grateful for it every time.

On Good Friday I stand in front of my congregation to witness to the death of Jesus. I look into the faces of our people, noticing anew all those who also are grieving. I hold myself firmly together until one of the closing hymns describes the pale, anguished brow of the Lord as he dies, and suddenly I see my grandfather's face again, pale and anguished, preparing to meet God, and I weep. When the service ends I exit out the back and walk to the side of the sanctuary where I can stand and cry alone, unnoticed. *Gently now.* This is the one service a year we don't have a greeting line with the pastor. I'm grateful for the space.

On Easter Sunday, we sing about resurrection and hope, the triumph of life over death, God's cosmic *yes* to all that we long for. All the while I hold the heartache of separation from a man I will never hug again on this earth. As Jackson, our senior pastor, preaches, I sit beside Daryl, one hand on his knee, and look out the window, trying to distract my tears. A deep blue bird I've never seen before perches on a tree in the prayer garden. As far as I can tell, it isn't a Mountain or Western Bluebird, a Scrub Jay, or a Blue Grosbeak. Its feathers are navy-royal and iridescent, its breast rufous, its beak delicate, its body round. It sits facing the big stone cross in the garden, not singing or preening but simply waiting, watching, alert and still.

I notice Jackson noticing me looking out the window, and I turn my attention back to the sermon.

"This kingdom began on Easter Sunday," he says, "but it will find its completion when Jesus returns."[5] I press a hand onto my heart.

When I look back for the bird, it is gone.

II

PEACE

DOVES

May our afflictions be few,
but may we learn not to squander them.

Scott Cairns

Doves are a near-universal symbol of peace. Ever since Noah sent one out of the ark and it returned with an olive branch, we've looked to doves as reminders that God is present to us and with us and within us. It was a dove that alighted on Jesus at his baptism, a sign of his anointing with the Holy Spirit, of God's delight in him. Doves mark our peace-themed seals and stamps and banners and art—Picasso's *Dove of Peace* was chosen in 1949 as the emblem for the first International Peace Conference in Paris as the countries of the world began picking up their shattered fragments after the Second World War.

But perhaps they shouldn't be held in such holy esteem. After all, there's no significant scientific or taxonomic distinction between an ethereal dove and a garbage-pecking pigeon. Doves build shoddy nests. They eat off the ground. Their primary predator is—get this—*rats*.

Doves are stout-bodied, short-necked, and loud, flappy fliers. Their wings' low aspect ratio allows them to take off in quick, short bursts, and their feathers' unusually loose attachment to the skin lets them seemingly disappear in a burst of fluff when threatened by predators.[1] Well, most predators. The last time Pope Francis released white doves after one of his weekly Angelus prayers, one was immediately attacked by a gull and another by a crow, leaving the crowd of worshipers aghast in a sea of feathers and the media buzzing with words like "omen."[2]

Come to think of it, maybe doves are the perfect symbol for peace.

One of my childhood pastors used to botch the Christmas Eve sermon every year, despite it being the second-easiest home run in the church calendar. All a preacher needs to do is mention at some point—any point—that Jesus was born and why it matters. The only sermon easier than this one is Easter Sunday. But inevitably the pastor would get in his head about doing something new, making it fresh, not just repeating the same pageantry of shepherds and wise men and angels being heard on high, and year after year he'd default to talking about his own family's bickering. One year he titled his sermon "Home for the Hostilities," and I thought my father, who is not a person who walks out of things, might stand up and leave.

"Maybe you aren't getting along with your spouse," the pastor said. "Maybe the kids are back from college and they're angry at you. Maybe it's time to bring God's peace into the home."

I could never figure out whether my dad was grumpy about the pastor's assumptions that all families were facing Yuletide turmoil or the annual swing-and-a-miss of the Nativity story, but in my teenage years I grew to appreciate the pastor's honesty about the rough go he was having in his own home, with his own adult children. It pulled back the curtain on the shiny, impossible perfection we expected of our spiritual leaders—*Pastors! They're just like us!*—and made me feel less alone as I watched my parents tie themselves in knots trying to keep Grandpa and Uncle Bill distracted enough through our festivities that their decades-long cold war wouldn't erupt into a huge fight. No sir, nothing to see here.

After the gull-and-crow incident, the pope's white doves were replaced by balloons,[3] which threw the Audubon Society into a tizzy because of the Vatican's assumption that polluting was somehow better than grisly bird drama. Jesus is born, we're all fighting, and the doves of peace have been replaced with airborne toxic plastic. We just can't get it right, can we?

But maybe this is part of the invitation of peace: to stop trying so gosh darned hard to make it happen ourselves and start looking to the one who can.

It's mid-July now, ninety degrees and as muggy as wet flannel as my grandmother and extended family and I stand awaiting military honors at a small, well-kept cemetery. It is so far from anywhere we've ever been that it feels, as my brother-in-law will say later, like driving into the center of nothing. I spent the first eighteen years of my life in northern Wisconsin, and I've never heard of this town. *Harshaw*. It sounds vaguely German or Polish, as many Wisconsin towns do. It's not much more than fields and forests, a gas station and a bar. Once again, we've all gathered, and we stand together in the beating sun.

Daryl and the kids are here, dressed in shades of blue and khaki, Lincoln mosquito-bitten and tanned from his morning at a summer camp in the woods. I'm going another round with laryngitis, a problem that's plagued me since early in ministry but grown worse with age and fatigue. This time I'm under a doctor's orders to rest my voice *completely*, so I'm parenting by whistle and whiteboard and wicked stare. My sisters, their husbands, their kids, and my parents are here. Grandma looks steady and ready in her wraparound sunglasses, her hair done in its usual Hepburn curls. My uncle and aunt are here with my two cousins standing skinny and blonde by their side. We are joined by a funeral director, an honor guard composed of seven men whose average age must be at least eighty, Grandma's priest, and a rotund, white-haired gentleman in a white shirt standing halfway up the grassy hillside behind the pergola. I can't tell if he's leering or land-scaping, but he's oddly placed. My dad gives the nod, and the honor guard begins.

"We are here to honor John Smith," the funeral director says, and beside me one of my sisters clears her throat. That isn't Grandpa's name. It's close, but not it. Grandpa has been spared many of the little indignities so common to death: he never had to endure transport to a rehab facility; he didn't die alone or in a nursing home; his hospital was new and clean; his doctor and nurses were kind. But today, at his funeral, he is called by the wrong name. I can't decide whether it matters or not. We all know who he is. God has always known.

The honor guard stands proudly and formally in the direct sun-light. Each of these elderly men gives of their time to stand in the baking heat or pouring rain or bitter cold to pay final respects to a serviceman or woman, a thought that makes me proud and sad. They read through their patriotic liturgy, short and sweet, and two walk to the center and unfurl an American flag, holding it up before us. "Taps" rings out on a bugle. It's the man on the hillside. Ah.

The men with the flag fold it into a neat triangle, their white gloved hands precise and unhurried in their task. The leader then presents it to my grandmother, with a word of gratitude from the president of the United States. My sons raise their eyebrows, impressed.

"That concludes this portion of the service," the director tells us, and we linger a moment in the hush. A song sparrow on the grassy hillside calls out. The honor guard walk crisply to their vehicles, leaving us behind. We slowly leave the pergola for the unshaded cemetery where neat rows of white tombstones stand vigil. There is a small, freshly dug hole awaiting my grandfather's ashes in their handcrafted wooden box, its latch made from a fishing bobber, a gift from a longtime family friend. We gather near, three-year-old Felicity deciding she's had enough and flopping down into the grass. Father Maria Joseph begins.

The words of his prayers wash over me, some familiar, others less so. We adults are an ecumenical bunch: two Presbyterian ministers, a Baptist pastor, the Evangelical Free folks, the Roman Catholics. The funeral director later tells us he is Missouri Synod Lutheran.

"Eternal rest grant unto him, O Lord," prays the priest. "And let perpetual light shine upon him. May he rest in peace."

The Protestants all keep going a few words too long during the Catholic version of the Lord's Prayer.

We take a few pictures, then we get in our cars and drive away, back to my parents' house.

The joke—well, one of many—about beauty pageants is that the answer to any hard-hitting question during the interview portion is always "world peace." It's such a pipe dream, such a fantasy, such a nonanswer to the real problems plaguing the world that it's become a trope.

I have not come to bring peace, says Jesus, *but a sword.* And we're ready for this, ready to strike down anyone in our path. We neglect the later portions of Matthew 10 where he reminds us that whoever does not take up their cross—an instrument of self-giving love—and follow him is not on the path at all. That whoever finds their life will lose it, and whoever loses their life *for his sake* will find it. The lack of peace Christ brings is not us at war against our neighbors or even our enemies, but the sword that pierces down to our very souls, dividing motive from action, love of self above all from love for Savior and neighbor and stranger and enemy. Peace is costly.

Yet peace is promised in our Holy Scriptures, and not—praise God—because it depends on us finally getting it right. Gentle Jesus, preaching what poet Mary Oliver calls his "melancholy madness,"[4] will be the one to lead us through. Not via conventional means, either. Neither warships nor roundtables will get us there. Instead, he promises that he himself is the way. I do not pretend to know what that means, except to say that my soul gets a little thrill whenever I think about it. Jesus as bridge, as highway, as Jacob's ladder, leading not only to our eternal rest but to the new creation, healed and whole.

This doesn't mean we are off the hook down here. Peace is a calling to each and every one of us. Within our homes, on our streets, in our communities. We work for peace at the community level, the state level, the national level. We work for international peace. Even if the work for some of us who lack power or influence or mobility or sway is prayer alone, we are to put hand to the plow and not look back. It is hard and holy work, and doves can help show us the way.

A pair of Mourning Doves regularly hangs out in our backyard. They might be nesting there, but it's difficult to tell. Dove and pigeon nests are usually no more than a handful of sticks thrown together in a loose pile. Some naturalists believe this is so their nests are easy to rebuild if they're knocked over by foragers or predators, but I think doves are just a wee bit lazy. Not in a slovenly, couch-potato way. More of a "life's tough and I'm kinda tired" way. Anytime a rainstorm or the neighborhood cat or a stiff wind breaks down the nests of the house finches, leaving them frantic and scrambling, I picture the Mourning Doves nodding to one another and saying, "See, Marge? I told you we shouldn't belabor the nest thing. Give me half a minute and I'll have ours back together."

Their wings whistle when they explode into flight, an exercise that takes a great deal of energy and effort. No wonder ours spend most of their time on the ground or atop our stone fence, placidly puffed up and occasionally cooing a warning if a hummingbird wanders too close. While our sparrows and House Finches jostle for best positions on the feeders, the doves simply hop down to the ground beneath and wait for whatever shakes loose. There's a sagely patience to doves. A placid hardiness.

The dove and pigeon grouping, a single family—*Columbidae*—boasts 310 species in forty genera worldwide.[5] There are doves as big as turkeys and as small as House Sparrows, doves with brightly colored plumage and those that are solid matte gray. Some sport flamboyant crests, others soft, smooth crowns. Doves feature uniquely shaped feathers on round-tipped wings, fluffy breasts, and necks that are often as iridescent as a hummingbird's. They live in every single country on earth and every continent but Antarctica.

They thrive in even the most gnarly, industrialized city spaces and can be found everywhere from dense jungles to prairie grassland. They are adaptable, stout, sturdy, and vocal.

They're also one of the only birds that can drink water without tilting or lifting its head, perhaps an adaptation borne from their general lack of predators. No need to keep a lookout when no enemies are on the horizon. Gideon would not be pleased.

Doves show up in Greek mythology as a sign of love and peace. They're particularly associated with the goddess Aphrodite, and they are often depicted as flocking to or around her. In the *Epic of Gilgamesh*, a story is told of a worldwide flood that culminates in the hero, Utnapishtim, releasing a dove from the boat he's built in order to discern whether there is any dry land to be found. (Sound familiar?) Doves show up as a sign of peace in Mesopotamian, Syrian, and Native American mythology as well, though interestingly, in Japanese mythology doves are most closely associated with Hachiman, a god of archery and war. (Perhaps this is where the Royal Air Force got the idea to use the dove as its symbol for tactical communications—clearly just a *peacekeeping* thing.)

To speak of peace in times of war and tumult and crisis and violence can seem foolish.[6] Hopelessly nostalgic. As out of touch with reality as the viral video of a woman *filming her workout* while tanks and armored vehicles amassed behind her, the beginnings of a coup in Myanmar.[7] We must reckon with our propensity toward discord and violence or our words of peace will ring hollow. As author Octavia Butler put it, "The world is full of painful stories. Sometimes it seems as though there aren't any other kind."[8]

The prophet Jeremiah cautions against those who lie about how deep our injury goes:

They dress the wound of my people
    as though it were not serious.
"Peace, peace," they say,
    when there is no peace.[9]

Throughout the Old Testament, prophets speak of a coming king who will bring true and lasting peace, not through war or violence but through justice and mercy and righteousness. As N. T. Wright puts it, "When God wants to take charge of the world, he doesn't send in the tanks. He sends in the poor and the meek."[10]

In Isaiah 9, the prophet proclaims that the instruments and weapons of hatred—every boot used in battle, every garment rolled in blood—will be fuel for the fire. When I first heard this passage as a girl, the imagery seemed ancient and far off, remnants of an uncivilized, ancient time. Surely, we'd moved past this. Now I see these boots and bloody garments on the evening news and know how close to home they really are. Our hope must come from outside our own crooked hearts. Isaiah paints a picture of the lasting peace only God can usher in, a kingdom where the trappings of war will be so useless that they will serve only to keep us and our neighbor warm in the winter's chill. Isaiah proclaims the truth: the peace we need comes from God. As W. H. Auden wrote in his "Christmas Oratorio," "Nothing can save us that is possible."[11]

The aching reality is that the battle lines of violence and fear, suspicion and bitterness, death and destruction are not just *out there*. They run right through the center of each beating human heart. Through mine. Through yours. Through our lowest impulses and our secret sins as we choose who we will serve, this day and every day. As we choose, much more often than we should, to serve and honor our idols. Even when we work to follow the rules, we often miss something. "When we choose the rule rather than the intent behind it, it can become an idol," noted our worship leader Jeff, pausing between songs one Sunday morning. Legalism is no substitute for a relationship with the living God.

Peace comes to us in different clothing than we may expect. It owns no fighter jets. It has no defense budget. It does not engage in debates online. In it comes, like poet Carl Sandburg's fog, "on little cat feet."[12] Meek and mild, holding a cup of cold water in the guise of a child. This does not mean it is weak—far from it. The peace spoken of in Scripture, borne in the body of Jesus on the cross, is stronger than any weapon we can fashion, more powerful than hatred, destruction, wickedness, or violence. Its power is love, and love, Scripture tells us, never fails. Why? Because God is love. *He himself is our peace,* Ephesians teaches.

Still, we may look around and ask, where is this peace? These last painful years have laid bare our many foibles and failings. The word *apocalypse* actually means "unveiling," and the revelation of so much so quickly has left me breathless. I thought I knew my country. I thought I knew my neighbors. I thought I knew myself. But naivety is not the way to peace. It is not through unknowing or passively acquiescing that we will find an answer to brutality and evil and violence. We cannot plead ignorance when we are part of the problem and, deep down, we know it.

And yet in this bloody and broken world, birds sing out the truth and mountains point to the truth and poets and prophets and artists hold up their words and their images and their paintbrushes and beckon. The Prince of Peace is coming. He has come, and he will come again. The peace that transforms our understanding is gently, quietly, persistently drawing ever closer.

When all looks lost, when all looks cold and still and hopeless and done for, when it's already the depth of winter and we are looking down the long tunnel of an aching Lent, the seeds that

God scattered when all seemed lost begin to sprout in the darkness underground. When evil looks as though it finally has the upper hand, there is, as C. S. Lewis wrote, a deeper magic at work.

I am hungry for the solving of all things. However the arc of the universe may bend, it is taking too damn long. The sins we have done and the sins done against us threaten to unravel not only each one of us but the very fabric of the cosmos. How can there be peace on earth when this very morning I was at war with our recalcitrant coffeemaker, not to mention our neighbor who loves his 11:00 p.m. fireworks all summer long?

"Then in despair I bowed my head," the centuries-old Christmas hymn goes. "There is no peace on earth, I said. For hate is strong and mocks the song of peace on earth, goodwill to men."

Maybe the answer isn't that our dreams are too big or God's answer too slow to arrive. Maybe peace comes like nearly every other good thing: tiny and imperceptibly at first, a seed sown in good soil, a fragile sprout curling its way up to the light, springing up under our feet even now. A seed too small to be of any use on its own but holding within it the power of life. The power of God.

In times of despair, the birds point me back to God. "The story isn't over yet," they remind me, as they keep building nests.

His word is love and his gospel is peace.

A number of years ago a man opened fire at a synagogue near San Diego. It was the usual—oh, God, it's become *usual!*—horror: unhinged gunman, unprovoked attack, innocent civilians. But one particular fact stood out to me. The young man who committed this act of terrorism was a Presbyterian. A member of good standing in his local church. And then I thought immediately of the synagogue right down the street from ours. How must it feel to its leaders and congregants to have a tall steeple church of the same denomination just a few blocks away? The rabbi at our synagogue knew the murdered woman personally. I had to stop myself from picking up the phone to call and justify myself and all our members—*Not all Presbyterians. We love you very much. You don't have to worry about us.*

Then I realized—before picking up the phone, thank God—that I'd be putting the burden of comfort squarely on the grievers. It is good and right to allow grief to flow in its natural direction—outward, from those whom it affects most. Never should those closest to a tragedy be expected to assuage the guilt or comfort the sadness of those who are only tangentially connected to the crisis. No one needs an emotional vampire when they're simply trying to put one foot in front of the other. If I was to call at all, it should only be to extend our condolences and support.

I rang the office and the rabbi's wife answered the phone.

"I am so sorry this happened," I said, after initial pleasantries. "I want you to know that my church and our pastors care about you and your congregation. Is there anything we can do to bless you?"

I realized at that moment that even asking the question was placing the burden on her to think of something for me to do. (We bumble in our efforts so often, don't we?) There was a long pause.

"Thank you," she said. "Thank you for calling. I appreciate the offer of help, but rather than you helping us, we would love it if you would come and join us for services. The memorial is in two days. Just come and be our guests."

So we did, me and a handful of congregants. I donned my clerical collar, pastoral pageantry I rarely pull out in our informal California culture, but a visual symbol that would immediately point me out as the pastor who'd phoned. I sat on the women's side of the divided sanctuary, quickly getting lost in the lengthy prayer books. Several worshipers behind me extended gentle hands to guide my reading.

"It took me years to figure all this out," one stage-whispered. "Don't worry. It gets easier."

Together we stood and sat and prayed and sang and listened as the rabbi eulogized the murdered woman, her faith and service, her mission for peace. He reminded us that her work remained unfinished and that God was with us in the struggle. She wouldn't be forgotten. Neither would we.

After services we were ushered over to tables laden with food and drink.

"Thank you for being our guests," the rabbi said, coming over to me with a smile. "Please, join us again."

I wondered why I'd served a church just down the street from this synagogue for nearly a decade without visiting once. I remembered experiences visiting churches around the country and how rarely I was welcomed with the same sort of open arms and unbridled delight I'd experienced among these Jewish worshipers— and today of all days, as we remembered a woman shot to death by one of our Presbyterian brothers.

Everyone in the family has an opinion on Grandpa's final destiny. Grandma maneuvered him into receiving last rites from Father Maria Joseph ("I just told him it was a blessing") and has poured much of her fixed income into the coffers of the Catholic church, convinced these contributions had him out of purgatory by Easter.

Those in our midst who lean more evangelical are haunted by uncertainty. Grandpa never prayed The Prayer or said The Words or pledged any Divine Allegiance. It gnaws at them, and some say as much. They want proof. Assurance.

I'm basically paid to weigh in on eternal matters, and yet when my oldest son asks, "Was Grandpa a Christian?" I can't say. That certainty is God's alone. But here is one thing I know beyond doubt's shadow: God loved my grandfather.

Grandpa lived a lonely and brutal childhood. He never knew his father. His mother sent him to rural Wisconsin to live with his grand-parents when he was still a boy. He had no siblings. I only heard him speak of his mother once, his voice so rigid with pain I never asked about her again. I know she was absent. I fear she was cruel.

When we buried my grandmother's mother over a decade ago, we were standing together in a wet Chicago cemetery saying our goodbyes when Grandpa began quietly walking along the rows and rows of inurnments.

"I think my mother is here," he said. I walked beside him for a few moments, reading the names on the other side of the aisle, intent on helping if I could. Then the family began packing up for the car.

"It doesn't matter," he said. "We can go."

I simply don't believe that God witnesses all the ways we've been pressed down until we shatter and then stops loving us because we never figured out how to mend those broken places. My grand-father could never really hear God clearly within the walls of a church, through the voice of a pastor or a priest. He never bowed to Grandma's constant pressure to attend Mass, though if the weather was bad, he would drive her there and wait in the car. Grandpa couldn't find God in any of the conventional ways, whether through choice or ability—and, really, aren't we all an amalgam of both?—so God did what God always does. God con-tinued speaking, but in other voices.

When I was a young girl, I read and reread The Chronicles of Narnia series. Jesus often seemed odd and remote, vaguely immodest hanging up there on the cross in his loincloth—but Aslan, the great golden lion? Aslan and I understood one another. I watched God reach out to my grandfather through the chickadees at his window feeder. I watched my grandfather pull on his blaze-orange knit cap and trudge down the snowy hill to the lake, drilling holes through the thick ice in an effort to hook the northern pike God had set in the waters below. God sent speckled fawns in spring and hummingbirds in summer and one special autumn, a black bear. Two weeks before my grandfather died, the first wild turkey came to sit atop his porch railing.

I don't know if Grandpa would have connected any of it to God. He was a man of few words, and fewer of those vulnerable or sentimental. He would have been at home in the Psalms, I think. Jeremiah. Job. Ecclesiastes. But people had let him down a time too many. From his earliest days, life taught him to layer steel around his heart to survive.

A few days before my grandfather died, my father spoke to him of eternity, Grandma chiming in that in the afterlife he'd get to see his mother and her mother—whom he never really liked that much—and Grandpa gazed off into middle distance.

"And Laddie," he said, naming the German shepherd he'd raised forty-some years earlier. "And Dusty." A black Labrador. "And Thisby." A gray tabby.

Consider the birds, said Jesus, and my grandfather did.

Come to me, you who are weary, Jesus said, and my grandfather was.

People press my hand at funerals all the time and ask for answers. Assurances. Certainty. We all sometimes imagine that these are the same thing as peace. They are not. I may have known a person's loved one well for years and years, or I may have never even met them, but I always offer the only peace I have to give:

God loved him very much, I tell them.

Jesus died for her.

The Spirit was present to them.

I want my worst mistakes to be of tenderness and grace. In all my wanderings with Jesus, I've never been able to imagine him as someone who wouldn't rush to welcome broken souls.

For God so loved the world, Jesus tells us, *that whosoever believes . . .*

What is belief but hope tethered to the desire for a deeper, better, gentler, truer way? As Madeleine L'Engle wrote, "I don't have any answers here, just a lot of questions and hopes, about a God of love who prefers parties to punishments."[13] Jesus calls it the kingdom of heaven. I'm no universalist, but I hold hope for all those who live with this longing. I believe we can trust those we love to the love of God.

If doves are just pigeons by another name, and Jewish worshipers can welcome the Presbyterians from down the street after a fatal shooting, if men who never knew their fathers are visited by chickadees in the waning afternoon as an offering of grace and peace they can receive, if the kingdom of God comes through the meek and the mild and the mustard seed, then maybe—just maybe—there's hope for us all.

12

LOVE

PELICANS

What is unnamed is often unnoticed.

Eugene Peterson

After my grandfather's memorial we sit on my parents' back deck and tell stories.

Grandpa served in the military.

One of my brothers-in-law doles out fried fish he caught, cleaned, and battered himself, bluegill and walleye, and we eat together in the mugginess of the late afternoon.

He always used a bandanna as a handkerchief and kept it in the back pocket of his jeans. After using it, he'd put it right back in that same pocket. Ew.

My uncle and cousins wear Heileman's Old Style T-shirts; a cooler is stocked with this, Grandpa's favorite beer.

He loved the woods.

I brought more fancy chocolates from California, my grandmother's favorite, in hopes that their sweetness can assuage the

emptiness of her house and her days. We pass one box around to
share and package up the rest to send home with her.

*He was a man of few words. He loved to sit by the big picture window and
look out at the lake.*

I'm still voiceless, so I type out the story I wish to tell, and Daryl
reads it from my phone.

*I remember what Grandpa said when I called to tell him I was going to
marry Daryl. Grandma said, "Oh, how wonderful." And then she gave the
phone to Grandpa, and I told him and there was a long pause.*

Daryl keeps reading.

There was a long pause and then he said, "Well, he'd better not be a shithead."

Chuckles spread through the patio chairs.

And Courtney felt very loved.

In early and medieval Christianity, the pelican became a symbol for
Jesus. Pelicans show up in stained glass windows and church statues
and religious iconography all over Europe. In Germany's Aachen
Cathedral, a blue, gold, and white mosaic shows a mother nurturing
her three chicks, colloquially known as "a pelican in her piety."

This odd bird seems a strange choice for a Christ figure, but the
idea originated in another ancient bird myth. Someone noticed a
Dalmatian pelican feeding her babies and, due to the way she
rested her pointed beak against her red-and-brown mottled breast,
mistakenly thought she was nourishing them with her very own
blood. (Very Julian of Norwich.) Thus, the legend spread.

Even if they don't give their own blood as food for their young,
these odd birds—awkward miracles, all feathers and dinosaur
parts—are rich with lore and mystique. Their long pouched beaks
give them a droll air, and their spectral eyes look both judgmental
and sage. Pelicans are among the many birds that transform in

color as they approach breeding season, their faces and bills bright-
ening as a signal to potential mates that they are hale and healthy.
They are sociable, hunting in flocks and traveling in masses that
sometimes number in the hundreds. They breed in colonies,
looking out for one another in congregated nesting areas. When it
rains, they open their enormous beaks to the heavens to drink.

In 1958 a White Pelican named Petros became the unofficial
mascot of the Greek island of Mykonos.[1] Found injured and floating
in the waters near the island, he was brought ashore by a fisherman,
nursed back to health, and given a name. In Greek, *petros* can mean
"rock" or "stone," but it can also mean "grumpy." (This helps the
apostle Peter make way more sense.) For nearly thirty years, Petros
wandered the streets and alleys of the island as a free-range pet of
sorts, enjoying photos with tourists and occasional pats from children.

All was peace and love until Petros got itchy wings and took a
short excursion to the nearby island of Tinos. Pelicans aren't native
to these Greek isles, and his presence quickly created quite an attachment. The residents of Tinos decided to keep Petros. This
didn't go over well with the Mykonosians, who instituted a lawsuit,
which they won. The famed pelican was returned to Mykonos in
short order, where he lived out the remainder of his days.

Here in Orange County, we have both Brown and American
White Pelicans. The American Whites like to hang out in calmer
waters—the local marsh, the tidal flats—where they placidly scoop
up their dinners from the water as if their beaks were soup ladles.
The Brown ones are more adventurous. I often spot them flying in
formation over the ocean, headed somewhere on important pelican
business. They circle and then dive spectacularly for fish from as
high as sixty feet aloft. Brown Pelicans frequent Dana Point Harbor,
San Clemente Pier, and the rest of our Beach Boys locales (sing it
with me: *Doheny, San Onofre, Trestles, Del Mar . . .*).

My friend Kassy took me out for my first surfing lesson, and as I lay on my belly in the sunny swell, Brown Pelicans began to swoop down to catch their lunch barely an arm's length away. They are the smallest pelican subspecies, with wingspans "as little as" six feet.[2] But when those birds are circling your head it's like being in the presence of pterodactyls. Six feet is pretty long, especially if you yourself aren't much over five.

"This is a good wave coming," Kassy would tell me, ever the encouraging teacher. "You can paddle for it!"

I caught a few, all flat on my stomach, save one where I shakily made it onto my knees. When the board caught in the whitewash and sped toward shore, my face broke into a grin so wide it ached. I suddenly understood why teens and twenty-somethings stave off college to camp down by the swell. I'd never felt anything quite like that rush of power and freedom, even on just these tiny, barely-even-there waves at our beginner's spot. Surfing felt like skiing down a moving snowpack, like painting atop a canvas in motion.

Kassy was a great instructor, setting me up for wonderful, gentle rides toward shore.

"That's it!" she'd call. "Paddle!"

But mostly I didn't paddle. I just bobbed and watched, amazed at the birds popping up from the shallows with fish in their pouches, straining out the saltwater before swallowing them whole.

One after another they'd crash-land near my board, not only unbothered by the presence of surfers but unwilling to make any concessions on their preferred fishing positions. At moments I could practically brush their wings with my fingertips. I couldn't see a single fish beneath me, yet one after the other the pelicans ducked down to snag their meals, finding an abundance where I saw only swirling sand and seaweed and foam. I began to imagine the heaving belly of a beast in the murky depths. If I couldn't see the fish the birds were easily snagging just two and three feet beneath the waves, what else might be lurking under my longboard? Every year or so a great white is seen swimming through our shallows and the beaches close for a couple of days. Every decade someone gets their legs bitten off. I'm not afraid to meet my maker, but I'd much prefer not to be eaten on my way there. I paddled to shore.

That was my first and last time surfing. These days I've traded in my borrowed board in favor of hikes around a local marsh.

The thing about marshes is that they are shark-free. And they still have many pelicans.

I'm back at the doctor's office for my laryngitis, diagnosed with laryngopharyngeal reflux, known colloquially as "silent reflux" because it doesn't come with any easily observable symptoms. I'm still so hoarse I'm barely audible, awaiting results from another exam.

"We will double your medication," he tells me. "And you'll need to continue to rest your voice."

He is a kind man, the father of young children himself, and he notices when the tears spring to my eyes.

"I'm so sorry," he pauses in the doorway. "Chronic illness is very difficult."

I have no words, so I nod, reach for a tissue, fold my hands in my lap, and sigh.

It's the month before Daryl and I go on pastoral sabbatical for the first time, me after twelve years in ministry, him after eight. As we've told close friends, "It's either sabbatical or death by spontaneous combustion." It's a joke, but also we are both so tired we can see burnout approaching like a lumbering train. My exhaustion manifests physically, my voice breaking down to a reedy nothingness, my sleep patchy and disrupted, my eyes lined with fatigue. Daryl's comes out in impatience and despair, shortness with himself, with the kids, with the FedEx guy who keeps delivering the furniture we ordered for the church's youth room to the wrong address. We are the walking wounded, Daryl and me.

The last time I remember being this tired was when I went back to full-time ministry just six weeks after the birth of our oldest son, a rosy-cheeked, dearly loved child who absolutely refused to sleep more than an hour at a time. On Sundays Daryl would bounce the baby in the side room of the arched sanctuary while I shook congregants' hands after worship, my modest black dresses hiding the various tummy bands I wore to keep my postpartum insides from falling out, glancing surreptitiously at my watch now and then to estimate how much longer I could keep chatting before risking a milksplosion. Dear folks I'd ministered to and walked alongside for years, people I loved, would pause to tell me about their aunt's illness or the upcoming high school baseball game and I would smile and nod and think, "Oh, I don't care. Please stop talking so I can go nurse my baby and nap."

We got through it, all of us, but just barely, the bone-crushing exhaustion fading to normal parent-of-a-baby tired after another couple months of sleepless nights, but I never went back to full-time work that quickly after birthing again.

These last few years, after pastoring through a pandemic, a contentious election, a racial reckoning, and the rising age of misinformation, challenges have risen hard and fast. Daryl and I recognize that we are at the end of our vocational ropes. I'm grateful for our time of approaching rest—our senior pastor, board of elders, and congregation have given it willingly, graciously, happily. We could have requested it a year earlier, but the church was still reeling and pivoting on the outer edge of the pandemic. The timing now is better for them, but we are also at the brink of what we can give before we collapse. In our typical overachieving fashion, we wrote up a lengthy plan for continuing education—learn Spanish! write books!—and the personnel committee gently suggested that maybe instead we should just *rest*. God bless them, every one.

So here we are, on the cusp of three months' sabbatical. We will worship together with our congregation on Labor Day weekend and then step away until after Thanksgiving. I have words I want to leave with everyone before these months of absence, words of encouragement and comfort, challenge and calling forth. But instead, I am pastoring by text and email, wondering—at my lowest moments—whether my voice will ever be strong and stable enough to preach again.

"I feel so useless," I whisper to Daryl, and he assures me that I'm okay, that everything is okay, and I pretend to believe him as he reads bedtime stories to our children, explains to the neighbors why I am not returning their shouted greetings, and calls the pharmacy to refill my medication because I lack enough voice to be heard over the phone.

The children ask me questions to which the answers are nuanced, complex, but all I have is a nod or a head shake or a shrug. The younger two are not yet able to read my scribbled notes on the whiteboard I tote around like a talisman. Our oldest is a champion in helping me communicate, yelling our menu choices from the back seat while we're in the drive-through, patiently explaining a school flyer to his brother, relaying messages to the delivery person at the door, but he's also only nine years old and I don't want to lean too hard on him with my malady.

"Can I have another yogurt?" *Nod.*

"Is it okay if we watch *Iron Chef* before dinner?" *Head shake.*

"What time will daddy be home?" *Shrug.*

Without my words I feel unmoored, unseen. But I am also discovering new ways to listen. I am learning how vulnerability can engender compassion, how being strong and capable isn't always the best way to move through the world because being strong and capable can insulate us from the reality that we are all connected. Dependent. Built in and for relationship. Designed to need one another.

In line for coffee, a barista wishes me a good morning and I point to my throat and mouth the words, "Lost my voice."

"Oh gosh," she says, "that must be so difficult. Here, write down your order for me."

At McDonald's the next day the cashier runs to the back room to get me a pen and paper after my unsuccessful menu pointing. On a hiking trail, a man with a dog begins an exchange of pleas- antries before I whisper that my voice is gone.

"That happened to me once," he said. "It was gone for months. It was so difficult. I am really sorry. Hang in there."

I used to spend much of my hiking time making phone calls. Now, I walk silently through the California hills, mourning the things I wish I could say but also surprised by how many birds I'd been missing. There are goldfinches in the scrub, wrens atop the bushes, a whole swirling scene of crows over the canyon. I hear an unfamiliar song and check my app—it's a White-crowned Sparrow, back from its migratory journey. We can't talk and listen at the same time, after all, and almost all wisdom comes in the listening— to others, to the Lord, to the heartbeat of creation.

Margaret Atwood tells the story of going to a costume party with her partner Graeme Gibson, both dressed as Odin's ravens. "The names of these ravens were Huginn and Muninn—Thought and Memory—and they flew around the world during the day, returning in the evening to perch on Odin's shoulders and tell him what they had seen," she wrote. "This is how Odin became so wise: he listened to the birds."[3]

Brown Pelicans, described by the Cornell Lab of Ornithology as "comically elegant," are a fascinating study in resilience and community action.[4] Because they are heavier birds, up to eleven pounds, and they incubate their eggs basically by standing on them, the shells of those eggs need to be quite sturdy. The widespread use of pesticides such as DDT in the 1940s resulted in weakened eggshells, and within a few decades, Brown Pelicans were pushed to the brink of extinction in California and the southeastern United States. When Florida banned such toxins in 1970, the rest of the country soon followed suit, and the pelicans began to make a slow comeback.

People's love for pelicans—and other large birds like eagles that were threatened by these pesticides—proved salvific. In 2009 Brown Pelicans were removed from the endangered species list. Today they remain a species of "least concern," their numbers rebounded to a place of thriving. Like many environmental problems, the situation was dire but not hopeless. Concerned scientists raised the alarm and citizens ranging from hobby birders to coastal dwellers to commercial fishermen and women advocated for change. Never underestimate what love can do.

And sometimes it is lament that awakens us to love. The two aren't opposites, but friends.

The hopeful comeback of the Brown Pelican reminds me of one of the most paradoxical passages in all of Scripture: the Beatitudes. The Greek word for *blessed* can basically be translated "happy." And not as in future-happiness-maybe-someday, but active, current happiness. In *Jesus Through Middle Eastern Eyes*, Kenneth Bailey puts it this way: "They affirm a quality of spirituality that is already present." In other words, the "point is not exhortation for a certain type of behavior. . . . The first statement affirms a happy state that already exists. The second statement affirms a future that allows [us] even now to live a happy life."[5] So the poor in spirit are happy now, even as they await the fulfillment of God's kingdom that will bring them lasting joy and peace.

"Blessed are those who mourn," Jesus tells the crowds, "for they will be comforted." They are happy now, even as they hold hope for their final consolation in Christ. "Blessed are the poor in spirit, for theirs is the kingdom of heaven."

Most of us have been on the receiving end of unsolicited advice, especially when it comes to medical issues. We complain of arthritis or astigmatism or acne and are met with stories about health complications alleviated through magical potions of essential oils or drinking more water or praying just a little bit harder. But Jesus is not an advice giver. He commands or comforts or invites; there is never any *should*. The Beatitudes simply state what *is*. We are free to disagree.

In my own season of mourning, I do not feel blessed as much as I do weary and tender and sad. I wish things were different. Easier. Kinder. I text my grandmother and send her pictures of the hawk on my evening walk and the woodpecker at the library.

How are you? I ask.

Oh, you know, she responds.

I visit another specialist, one of the foremost otolaryngologists in California, because a retired surgeon congregant gently asked if he might make a referral for me. I'm floored by the kindness, and it turns out to be a turning point in my recovery. The new specialist determines I have a paralyzed vocal cord. He tells me I can speak as much as my weak, quavering voice will allow, sets me up with a vocal therapist who can help my healthy vocal cord learn to compensate for my struggling one, and schedules a raft of additional tests. Maybe it's nothing; maybe it's capital letter Serious.

I get blood drawn in preparation, and the phlebotomist is so gentle she nearly brings me to tears. There is a sensitivity borne from suffering, a new tuning in to the pulse of creation. Our pain binds us to the pain of others, breaks us open to gratitude, slows us to a more measured, transcendent pace. Grief can help us learn to see.

Perhaps this is what Jesus means by *blessed*.

People share things at funerals that they don't at any other time. Stories come to the surface. Apologies are given and received. The taciturn family member steps, trembling, to the microphone. A memorial service is a time to name our collective, communal grief and, in putting it to words, to help carry its burden.

Eugene Peterson put it this way: "Naming focuses attention. The precise name confers dignity." There is power in putting words to what we see and feel and know. It draws us together through laughter and story, in the telling of truth through shades of memory. Peterson continues:

> My most memorable experience of this came in naming birds. I have known what a bird was from an early age and could name a few of them—robin, crow, sparrow. The ones I named I noticed (not the other way around). I was aware that birds were in the air and bushes and trees but never paid much attention to them. Then I became a bird-watcher. I learned to observe the birds, not just to glance at them. Within a few weeks I was seeing an enormous variety of birds and noticing how extraordinarily different they were from

each other. And I began to be in awe of how much there was yet to know, and how long a lifetime I would need to arrive at a mastery, and to regret my late start. A new world had opened up right before my eyes: colors, sounds, flight patterns. But it had always been there. Why was I now seeing? In large part through naming.[6]

I knew my grandfather for thirty-nine years, but on the deck at my parents' home after the funeral, I learn the names for different facets of who he was. I see him through the eyes of my uncle and mother, in the empty place by the side of my grandmother, amid the steadfastness of my father and aunt who showed such compassion to him in his final years.

"John and I have a good understanding," my dad would say, showing up with Grandpa's favorite Subway sandwich, sneaking him the occasional bottle of gin. We were a teetotaling house until my youngest sister left for college—I remember my father drinking exactly one beer during my entire childhood, at a San Diego Padres game with a friend—so my dad bringing surreptitious alcohol to anyone was a tremendous act of love.

My sister Caitlyn tells the story of trying to buy Grandpa a final taste of his liquor of choice at the gas station near the hospital the morning before he died.

"I can't imagine what the cashier was thinking," she said. "There I am at eight in the morning, standing by the register telling her, 'I just *really need some gin.*'"

Love pays attention. God paints the sunset even if we don't pause at the sink to look up, leaving the dirty dishes a moment longer. Annie Dillard wrote, "Acts of beauty and grace are performed whether or not we will or sense them. The least we can do is try and be there."[7]

Love is specific. We can't love in general any more than we can hope in general. It demands an object, a witness. It is not the devil who is in the details but the Lord.[8]

In Charles Yu's astonishing novel *Interior Chinatown*, the protagonist, Willis Wu, is billed in his movies as Generic Asian Man, a trope of blended sameness custom-made for background acting. At first he seems like no more than this flat conceit. But his distinctive self is quickly visible to his love interest when she picks him out of the crowd because of his charm, distinct from every other background extra, despite their identical heights and haircuts.

I didn't fall in love with my husband because of his love for good guacamole and well-polished shoes, his California confidence, or the tender way he held my face in his hands the first time he kissed me. But in another very real way, I did. This is how we are loved, how all of God's people have always been loved. Peter mouthing off, Mary clinging tearfully, Nathanael scoffing—all loved by God in their specific personhood, dearly cherished as works in progress, beloved children, grace upon grace stitching together every molecule of their beings.

In seminary, my favorite professor used to ask his students why we'd chosen ministry.

"I just really like people," one replied.

"Really?" asked the prof. "Have you *met* people?"

Loving the idea of people is not loving people. Abstractions are easy; it's individuals who are difficult to love. Ask any child or spouse or parent. Ask any leader or pastor or teacher. Yet this is our call, our task, our privilege. Paul's "greatest of these" is by far the most difficult, by far the most rewarding.

In my earliest years as a pastor, I often felt paralyzed by the inadequacy of my love. I couldn't help everyone, save anyone, or make even my little corner of Wisconsin a better place in any significant and lasting way. Calling one shut-in to offer prayer and a listening ear wasn't enough if I couldn't call them all. Preaching a powerful sermon was an exercise in ephemera—by the benediction I was in a cold sweat wondering what I'd preach the next Sunday. Even shoveling the snow out front became a metaphor for futility—often more began falling before I'd even taken my gloves off inside.

Yet this is the grace of love. We cannot do it all, but we can do one tender thing, and that specific act of paying attention to another contains whole worlds. Fancy chocolates from California and gas station gin and the offer of a red bandanna handkerchief when our nose is running or our knee skinned. We can meet with a brother in his distress, witnessing and acknowledging his pain. We can extend dignity to a sister after the loss of her job. We can remember the anniversary of the day a friend became a widow. We can pick up the phone, send the email, offer the card, hold the hand. Sunday after Sunday my gift and goal is to stand before God's people and point us toward the truest thing I know—Christ has died, Christ is risen, and Christ will come again.

To love is to choose—this person, this life, this sacrificial early morning, this late-night listening ear, this pause at the mailbox to ask a neighbor how the surgery went. Unlimited options are not grace but burden. We cannot save the world, or even ourselves. But we can do one tender thing. And then another.

Like pelicans diving into the sea, each gracing us with only a moment or two, plucking a fish from the water, flapping away. A flash of transcendence. A reminder that we are loved.

Because the new specialist has determined that my reflux is under better control, I'm now allowed to drink a small amount of caffeine and alcohol, eat chocolate, and have an occasional snack after 7:00 p.m. The tests I'm scheduled for today will help us get to the bottom of why I have a paralyzed vocal cord. They may tell me I have breast cancer or throat cancer or multiple sclerosis, but my evening snacks are back and I'm pretty euphoric.

"How are you doing with this?" Daryl asked me a few nights ago after we'd put the kids to bed.

I grinned and held up a big bowl of popcorn.

"Yes . . ." he said. "But how are you *really* doing?"

"Honestly, if I have to choose between giving up snacking, caffeine, citrus fruits, tomato sauce, carbonated beverages, *and talking* or having MS, I'd probably take the MS."

He watched me for a moment to see if I was joking. I wasn't. I figure we'll all end up in wheelchairs if we live long enough.

I am hoping hard that it's just a short in the wiring, though, like a car battery that sometimes goes on the fritz. Maybe they'll find nothing in the scans and the doctor will shrug and write, "Unknown causes," and I'll just work around the on-and-off laryngitis. Maybe tomorrow my voice will come back and I can stop hearing about things like swallow tests, which, as it turns out, have nothing to do with the birds that swoop down on San Juan Capistrano and everything to do with whether you're medically allowed to eat food through your actual mouth.

I take a nap in the MRI machine, because Skittles aren't a good breakfast and fear of the unknown makes for a fitful night's sleep. And as I lie there with the bumping and whirring of magnets, I remember lying on the gray-painted pier that juts out between the lily pads into my grandparents' lake. I can hear the sound of Grandpa's rowboat gently clunking against the dock. The Wisconsin breeze is warm against my face, the sun glaring, my long, brownish-blonde hair draped across my neck where rivulets of sweat drip down to my shoulder blades and then fall, one by one, to the pier. I toy with the turquoise ruffles on the neckline of my bathing suit. I'm supposed to wear a life jacket when I'm out on the water, but my sisters are up at the house with my mom and my grandma, so there is no one here to tattle on me.

I hear a creak, a heavy step onto the pier, and I turn my head to see a pair of sturdy brown shoes stopped an arm's length away.

"Hiya, Court."

My grandfather bends down, a round Styrofoam container in his hands. "I'm going fishing. Want to join me?"

He sits on the rickety bench at the pier's end. It leans to the right a little more every year. I sit beside him, watching his first cast, his hook and its red-and-white bobber swooshing behind our heads and then sailing in an arc toward the middle of the lake before landing with a splashy *plink*. The bobber sits perky atop the gentle ripples.

I poke a finger into the rich black soil inside the Styrofoam, feeling around for a worm. There it is. I feel it inch and tug against the pad of my skin. I bend my finger and pull it loose, brushing away the crumbs of soil. It loops and bends in my palm, an earthworm the color of liver or milk chocolate pudding, ruddy brown, ancient as the sun.

"Does it hurt them?" I ask.

Grandpa lost the first worm to a sneaky fish, and he holds up his empty hook, reaching with the other hand for the container of worms.

"I don't know," he says, and I watch as he spears a fat worm, bending it in half so the hook can pierce it again and again. It writhes, twisting in on itself in the universal sign for agony. I begin to cry.

Grandpa casts the line back in. The bobber sits back atop the waves. The lily pads gently rise and fall.

"It hurts them," I say.

"Maybe," he says.

"I don't like fishing," I say. "It's mean."

"Where do you think your fish sticks come from?"

I ponder this. The worm in my palm has grown still, warming quickly in the sun.

"Well, you can't kill this one," I tell him. "I'm going to set it free. In the forest."

He watches me, his faded blue eyes regarding me behind blonde lashes. Grandpa can recite a long list of Things That Aren't Free. It includes water and toilet paper and electricity, and I know for a fact that these worms come from the bait store in town, where I imagine those shop owners, too, are just out to make a buck.

"Go ahead," he says.

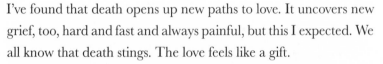

I've found that death opens up new paths to love. It uncovers new grief, too, hard and fast and always painful, but this I expected. We all know that death stings. The love feels like a gift.

Memories of my grandfather stick to me like forest burrs. I find them when I'm brushing my hair, pulling on my jacket, unwinding my scarf. Stories I haven't summoned in years come unbidden and stay awhile. I realize how much about him will now remain forever a mystery to me, but also how much more clearly I can see a rounded-out picture of who he was and how he shaped our family. His story's ending allows me to love him tenderly in memory in ways he didn't much allow in life.

When we die, we return to the dust, but we also return to those who loved us.

13

TRUTH AND BEAUTY

CORVIDS

Everything beautiful in this world is strange.

LADEE HUBBARD

AFTER GRANDPA'S FUNERAL, PEOPLE EAT and mingle inside and outside my childhood home. Photographs are displayed—Grandpa as a young man, Grandpa as a groom, Grandpa at the lake. There is a picture of him as a young father holding my mother, and as a young grandfather holding a fish. "8 lb 1 oz, 27" long," the caption reads, "1-7-92." It reminds me of a birth announcement. There's a recent one of him standing on the front porch of his house wearing his usual gray zippered hoodie and glasses, a navy blue baseball cap, a few layered T-shirts. He grips the railing with both hands—this photograph was taken after the surgery to amputate his lower right leg, a complication from diabetes. He is smiling. The sun shines on his face. He looks both eager and at ease. The smile is genuine, his eyes crinkled, his shoulders relaxed. This is how I picture him now. On a porch in the sun, at ease, smiling.

A black-and-white military photo catches my eye. Grandpa in fatigues, the khaki uniform of a private, a crisp garrison cap atop his head. His hands hang, curled loosely by his sides as he stands tall and full, with the half smile of an invincible teenage boy. He's on a street corner, and from the sliver of brick building I can see behind him, this must be Chicago. Grandpa enlisted at eighteen, right at the start of the Korean War, and was sent to serve as infantry in the Canal Zone down in Panama. In the pounding equatorial sun his fair skin would regularly burn to red blisters and his hair would bleach to near-white.

"Was Panama beautiful?" I asked him once.

"We had to shake scorpions out of our shoes in the morning," he told me. "Beautiful isn't the word I'd use."

We don't have Blue Jays in Southern California. We have Scrub Jays, their scratchy-voiced, rough cousins, but not the perfectly painted jays that reside almost solely to the east of the Rockies. Whenever I encounter a Blue Jay in my travels, I gasp. They are unearthly in their beauty with their illuminated, barred wings, their black bridles and necklaces, their sky blue backs and finely crested heads featuring feathers that rise and fall with their moods. Blue Jays look like stained glass windows, like tiny-winged cathedrals. I gasp at Blue Jays, and almost always, whoever I'm with at the time replies with some form of, "Yeah, but they're mean."

People don't tend to be lukewarm about Blue Jays. They love them or they hate them. This makes sense. Blue Jays *are* mean, if your definition of mean is making life generally miserable for other birds. Jays mimic the sound of hawks to drive competitors away from food or water; they steal; they pester; they dive-bomb. Blue Jays have been known to eat the babies of other avian species. They'll go through your garbage if you leave it uncovered. They're bully birds.

But here's the thing: Blue Jays are also really good at being Blue Jays. They form tight social bonds and close-knit family units. They sing screechily through the autumn months but are quiet in the spring during nesting season. They are smart enough to clean the bitter-tasting acid off ants and clever enough to survive in hawk-studded forests despite being the most visible prey. Blue Jays are intelligent, creative, and resilient. They speak their minds. You have to admire a critter for that. Monet once wrote that he wanted to paint the way a bird sings, and I can only imagine the riot of color and canvas a Blue Jay would require.

Blue jays are part of the corvid family, an avian subcategory that includes ravens, crows, magpies, jackdaws, and nutcrackers. These stout-billed, charismatic songbirds are known for being brilliant and devious, though arguably the latter is simply a result of the former. The class clown wasn't usually the dumbest kid in class; she was the one who was so smart she was bored. Corvids study and adapt to human behavior, fold seamlessly into suburban environments, and can even mimic the human voice.

Because corvids' habitat overlaps so closely with residential areas, nearly everyone has a story or two about them, birders and nonbirders alike. I remember a jay stealing half of my peanut butter sandwich on a childhood hike. While shyer or quieter passerines can fade into the background, corvids are conspicuous, standing out with both their voices and their behavior. Just this morning a family of five crows pulled a baby bottle out of my neighbor's trashcan and spent the morning presiding over their new prize with pride and curiosity, showing the bird that pulled it from the can special deference.

Corvids can be controversial. But perhaps beauty isn't as straightforward as we think, either.

I grew up with a gospel message centered on sin. We are fallen human beings, stuck in our own mess, so Jesus died on the cross to save us. This is not untrue, but it is an anemic version of a much fuller story. Circling around the idea of sin as the heartbeat of Jesus' message would be like describing my marriage as a union of two people who live together in the same house. This is true, of course; Daryl and I live in the same house, and this reality defines much of our ways of living and being. But it isn't what our marriage is *about*. It is infused with all manner of indescribable intangibles: love and compassion, commitment and care, honor and cherishing, empathy and listening, a thousand million kindnesses over the course of decades, the raising of children, the sharing of a bed, the calling to a church and a community. The house we live in affects us: how we live and love, what stressors we bear, what hospitality we can offer. But the house is not the main point. Similarly, the heartbeat of the gospel isn't our sin—it's the transformative, overwhelming, holy love of a Creator God for all creation. It is so much bigger and better—and more beautiful—than I'd been taught.

Going beyond the watered-down narrative or the moment-of-decision-driven story also makes room for an easier starting place when discussing things of faith with those raised outside the church. The sin-cross-salvation narrative makes little sense to the average person. *Sin? Cross? Atonement? Uh, sure.* People may get wigged out at a bloodied thirtysomething dying on a piece of wood, especially when the oft-cited reasons for such a gruesome death don't make a

lick of sense upon first reading—*God died to make things right with God?*
Really?—but I don't know that I've ever met a person who didn't
understand that things aren't as they should be. Death and violence
and illness and disaster have derailed so much of what we hope for.
Even the most perfect moments of our lives are less than flawless.
We can rarely even eat lunch outdoors without feeling too hot or too
cold or swatting mosquitoes. We long for wholeness, for peace, for
a world made new and right and good. Enter natural theology.

Natural theology teaches that God can be known, at least in part,
from creation. It's rooted in passages like Romans 1, where Paul
draws out the connection between the natural world and God's
character. If God can be reliably encountered in creation as both
the first cause of all created things as well as the highest example
of the many goodnesses we witness there, then exploring, enjoying,
and studying the natural world become unique acts of worship.
This line of thinking eliminates the false dichotomy between faith
and science, inviting us to view creation as one more window into
the heart of God.

Beyond this, I believe that which points us toward truth and
beauty cannot help but also point us to God. A healthy view of and
connection to nature gives us a gateway to the divine, a unique
perspective and understanding. We see this throughout Scripture—
the Psalms are bursting with natural imagery; Jesus regularly uses
agrarian references; the final resting place of the people of God is
described as a city, but one that includes a river and a tree—
harmony between humans and nature. It also humbles us as
stewards—those tasked to "live gently on the earth," as Christian
environmentalist Kyle Meyaard-Schaap puts it.[1]

Natural theology shows us that Blue Jays are really good at being
Blue Jays because the world was set in motion with goodness and
order. It does not teach that nature itself is God but instead that

creation points toward the existence of God based on observable facts. While we may not be able to describe the Trinity or an atonement theory based on galaxies and Galapagos Tortoises, we can look at either and learn broad, deep truths about how the world works and, by extension, about the God who spun that world into being. The specifics and particulars come to us through Scripture and the revelation of the Holy Spirit, but creation also testifies.

I grew up with Gnostic-adjacent theology. Bodies were not inherently evil, but they were certainly troublesome (lust! injury! hunger! but mostly lust!) and best used simply as tools, convenient carrying cases for the soul. Creation was fine—we could enjoy sunny days and fresh snowfall and puppies and kittens—but it was eternity that mattered. This is all too common in the modern church, particularly evangelical Protestant circles. We left behind a good deal of our robust natural theology during the Reformation, and now we wonder why we feel so impatient and unmoored, why our eschatology is all about "going to heaven someday," which isn't, in the end, even scriptural. N. T. Wright describes it this way:

> The first Christians believed not that they would "go to heaven when they died," but that, in Jesus, God had come to live with them. . . . The book of Revelation ends, not with souls going up to heaven, but with the New Jerusalem coming down to earth, so that "the dwelling of God is with humans." . . . What then was the personal hope for Jesus' followers? Ultimately, resurrection—a new and immortal physical body in God's new creation. But, after death and before that final reality, a period of blissful rest. . . . "In my father's house," Jesus assured his followers, "are many waiting-rooms." These are not the final destination. They are the temporary resting-place, ahead of the ultimate new creation.[2]

This realization helps ground us in our understanding of the work before us. Christians don't practice holy escapism; we are invited into real kingdom work here and now. Not in a guilt- or shame-based way, but like a gardener who cracks open the door to the outside and gestures, shovel in hand, to a blossoming, blooming yard, saying, "Come on out. There's good work to be done."

We are meant to be tethered to the earth. Our worship is not designed to be spiritual escapism or future-dreaming, but instead a way of rooting the love and justice of God more deeply into our hearts and rooting our feet more deeply into the soil of holy ground. As Ellen Davis puts it, "Worship is a vigorous act of re-ordering our desires in the light of God's burning desire for the wellness of all creation."[3]

Creation, then, has lessons to teach us about the rhythms and truths of the gospel, and vice versa. When we look at a Blue Jay, bold in its behavior, brilliant in its color, we are seeing something of the divine revelation, too. According to Thomas Aquinas, "Corporeal creatures according to their nature are good."[4] Trees are transcendent in their tree-ness. Dogs in their dog-ness. (Aristotle has a lot to say about this, but I won't do that to you. Daryl, on the other hand, would be happy to give you those footnotes.) This applies to the woods and wilds, but it applies to you and me, too. Every inch of skin, every blood cell, all our fingers and toes and nerves and sinews.

The more deeply I commune with the natural world, the more I see God both within and without. This isn't pantheism; it's praise. Jesus tells us that if we keep silent, even the stones will cry out. For so long, I was silent. Worse, I was unseeing. In Matthew 13:15, Jesus quotes Isaiah's warning, that even when we see, we will remain sightless:

For this people's heart has become calloused;
>   they hardly hear with their ears,
>   and they have closed their eyes.

Daily banquets of goodness and beauty are laid out before us. The world is afire with the goodness of God, if only we would look up.

Birds are some of my best teachers. Maybe yours are your garden or Labradoodles or the orchids that grow in the jungles of Costa Rica. Saint Augustine is a faithful guide into natural theology. He writes: "Question the animals that . . . fly in the air; their souls hidden, their bodies evident; the visible bodies needing to be controlled, the invisible souls controlling them; question all these things. They all answer you, 'Here we are, look; we're beautiful.' Their beauty is their confession. Who made these beautiful changeable things, if not one who is beautiful and unchangeable?"[5] A beautiful creation points to a beautiful Creator. Embodied theology is the only kind we have.

At the start of our sabbatical, Daryl and I visit the Getty Museum in Los Angeles and stroll through its exhibit of fourteenth- and fifteenth-century European religious art. Painting after painting features an act that strikes me as profoundly beautiful: the Virgin Mary breastfeeding. There is top-half nudity on every wall in sight, and nearly every single one of these paintings formerly hung in a church. *Bodies are good*, they sing to me from the museum walls. *Bodies are holy*. It takes me back to nursing my own babies when I so often felt the grumpy gaze of others questioning the appropriateness of my choice of location.

"Can't you do that in the bathroom?" an older gentleman once asked me as I sat in a restaurant booth, out of the house for the first time in days, my son's legs kicking happily from under the shawl I used as a cover. No one could *see anything*. But the simple reminder that I was a woman with breasts—used not for any sexual purpose in those moments, but instead to nourish a child—was often more than passersby could stomach. But natural theology reminds us that we, too, are creatures. We, too, are created by the God who designs beautiful things with beautiful purposes in mind. Birds—and bodies—are holy things.

My friend Anna invited me on a hike with a group from her church one autumn, seven or eight of us tromping through the fall foliage in western Massachusetts over a carpet of golden leaves and under a canopy of such bright, autumnal color the sky fairly glowed.

"Feel the ground beneath your feet," she said, and we did. "See what else you notice," she said, and we did. Above us, darting and circling through the chestnut and evergreen and maple trees were blue bursts of activity. Bird screams split the air: *Jay! Jay! Jay!* They were pestering a nuthatch; they were pestering a family of White-throated Sparrows; they were pestering a Dark-eyed Junco. And they were beautiful.

Blue Jays may not be good to other birds, but they are very good at being themselves. And this is its own kind of beauty.

Photographs freeze details for us, inviting contemplation like a painting. Every half decade or so when my sisters and I were young, my mother would pull yellowed photo albums off the shelves and ask my grandparents about their stories, about how they met and what they were like as teenagers and children and young adults. At the time this seemed as interesting to me as yard work; I'd look for an escape to the toys in the basement or the lake out back. Mom would summon us over to see and we'd feign interest before fading back to our activities. I wish I'd listened.

It takes seasoning to recognize the beauty in an ordinary family afternoon over photo albums and shared stories. I spent so much of my youth longing to escape what was right in front of me for bigger and better things. I realize now that bigger and better and beautiful don't often go together. The miracle is in the feather. The leaf. The acorn.

Scholars believe that the oak forests of the East were largely seeded by Blue Jays. Fond of these seedpods, Blue Jays litter the forest floor with them in their raucous meals. Slowly, year by year, the forests spread north and west, planted unintentionally by the brassiest of birds. They had no plans to create the habitats they did. But God knew.

I pause in my parents' living room now, in the aftermath of the funeral, and look at the photographs. Grandpa with another fish—a Northern Pike, I think. Grandpa with his beloved German Shepherd, Laddie. Grandpa with his children, bundled against a Chicago winter. Grandma and Grandpa at their wedding, him thin and proud-shouldered in a white coat, her with a tiny waist in a lace dress, dark curls set just so, fashionable eyeglasses, a coy smile. I see my uncle in Grandpa's face; I see my mother; I see my sister Caitlyn, who favors their side of the family the most. I see two hands poised to cut a cake, his over hers. I see laughter in both my grandmother and my grandfather's eyes, whole forests present in a tiny acorn of possibility.

I realize in this moment that my grandfather was a beautiful person. I realize, maybe for the first time, that there isn't any other kind.

There's a gopher skull on my writing desk, a gift from a farmer philosopher friend. I planned to name it Gomer—our church was camped out in the book of Hosea when I received the little cardboard parcel on my doorstep—but the farmer's son insisted on Greta because he was certain that whatever led the gopher to her demise caused her many regrets. Every writer needs a *memento mori*.

The skull arrived in a Ziploc bag nestled inside a newspaper-cushioned box, picked fairly clean by scavengers but still in need of a little care and polish. I cured it in boiling water—more gently this time than with my failed mockingbird experiment—and then soaked it in hydrogen peroxide, scrubbing it gently with toothbrushes, cotton swabs, and my children's old paintbrushes until it was clean and pristine, ready to spray with lacquer and dry in the sun. I hadn't held an animal bone from anything but a rotisserie chicken in decades (save for that sad mockingbird). This gopher's skull, small enough to fit in my palm, captivated me with its fragile arches and entryways, its delicate canals made for veins and vesicles, its long, yellowed, curved teeth.

Frederick Buechner died not long ago. Rarely a day goes by when I don't think of his instructions for living: *Here is the world. Beautiful and terrible things will happen. Do not be afraid.* This little rodent's skull sits as a reminder of the beauty and terror that make up every inch and atom of who we are. It's my nod to author Rachel Held Evans, whose writing desk featured the scribbled reminder: "Tell the truth."

Some birding magazines emphasize the beauty of birds over all else—*aren't they just so nice*—but stripped of their grit and gravity, birds are as boring as plastic flowers. Truth is *interesting*. A few months into my nascent hobby, I joined the American Birding Association and began receiving their magazine, titled simply *Birding*. I opened my first copy to an article on how incredibly frustrating it is to try to see—much less photograph—a Black Rail. These notoriously shy birds lurk at the bases of shoreline reeds and cattails, blending seamlessly into the shadows.

"*Yes*," I whispered. "*More of this.*"

The temptation to sanitize or anesthetize or oversimplify is strong. We run to hagiography, to pleasantries and, worst of all, to niceness. It doesn't take a very close reading of the Gospels to realize Jesus wasn't *nice*. He didn't glad-hand or work a room or turn on the charm. The truth can be a shock. Not in a bombastic, rude way—spare me the theobros who are caustic and aggressive for its own sake—but like a jolt of cold mountain water on feet that have grown hot and blistered during a long hike.

Perhaps it was because I was such an earnest, anxious child, so quick to tears, that the rural dentist I frequented as a youngster never drilled far enough when I needed a cavity repaired. The second I began to wince in pain, he'd stop.

"There!" he'd say. "We did it!"

In the moment, I was always grateful to have it over and done with. Fast-forward twenty years. Daryl and I were cash-strapped newlywed graduate students subsisting on beans and rice. I developed a toothache, so I visited a kind, soft-spoken dentist who took x-rays, pulled them up on his computer screen, and drew a sharp breath inward.

"I'm not sure how to tell you this," he said, "but there is decay under every single filling you have. We will need to redo every one."

As I absorbed the shock of what this would mean for my mouth and our bank account, he continued. "We will first fix the one that's causing you pain. Then we can do the others, a few at a time. Don't be afraid. We will go slowly."

The truth can be a shock, but it's also the only path to healing.

Crows will eat anything. They're the goats of the bird world, happy to ingest fruit, bugs, seeds, and any trash humans leave lying around. With their black bills, feet, eyes, and bodies, they are frequently seen as forbidding omens.

The crow that we spot often in our yard has one bright white feather on his flank—a unique but not unheard-of variation. We've named him Joe and the kids say hello to him as we bundle out the door to school in the mornings. Late one summer Joe perched on our apple tree, never breaking eye contact with me as he plucked the only remaining apple from its branches, spread his wings, and flew off.

"Pretty sure someone just put a spell on you," a friend quipped.

Crows may not be wicked—best not to ascribe morality to creatures who are just out there being creaturely—but they are wicked smart. Crows can recognize human faces. They use tools. Some scientists believe they have the same "cognitive toolbox" as apes.[6]

"You can train a raptor," Terry the owl lady told me, "but if you try to train a corvid, it will end up training you." These sneaky, observant birds coexist easily with humans, often preferring urban spaces to rural ones. Corvids help break down our nature/city dichotomies, reminding us that creation's gifts extend beyond the wilds. The delights of flora and fauna aren't just found on the hiking trail or the camping trip. Crows are a consistent reminder of the avian world because there are a heck of a lot of them. Writes Lyanda Lynn Haupt in her book *Crow Planet*, "For the majority of people on the face of the earth, the crow will be the single most oft-encountered native wild animal in their lives." There are an estimated thirty-one million crows in the United States alone.[7]

(Just to put that in scale, House Sparrows, the most ubiquitous birds on earth, number just seven million in the United States.)

Often when a word or phrase is repeated in Scripture, it's done so for emphasis. I wonder what the Creator may be trying to tell us with all the crows.

My friend Mark once served as a resident adviser at a Christian college, miffed that all his fellow RAs chose to decorate their dorm hallways with Bible verses and quotes from C. S. Lewis and Billy Graham.

"What'd you use?" I asked him.

At age nineteen, still holding tightly to every strand of fundamentalism I could muster, I still believed that these were *by far* the best choices.

"Annie Dillard."

Mark was an artist, miffed by how quick the rest of us were to shove God into a theological framework with no room for whimsy. It was Annie Dillard who wrote that we should be wearing crash helmets in church if we really believed all the wildness we preached about the truth and power of the Holy Spirit. As I've grown up into my beliefs, into psalms and parables and poetry, not just prescription and prohibition, it is Dillard's careful eye to the wild and wooly sides of nature that has done more for my faith than almost any sermon I've ever heard—or preached.

My paternal grandparents are faithful Presbyterians. For decades they attended a tall steeple church in Peoria that we couldn't step foot into without pantyhose and preparation to say the word *debtors*. My mom's mother is a devout Catholic whose congregation featured shushing and kneeling and candles I wasn't allowed to blow out. Perhaps it is unsurprising that I always felt most at home on Grandpa's quiet pier, nestled in lily pads and smeared with fish guts. There was something that rang true about his quiet gaze at the lake or the fire, his cranky declarations that so-and-so was being a shithead, his pronouncements that we should watch our wallets or our backs. Rare words wrenched out of him at moments of family intensity had a particular power and surprisingly incisive edge of prescience. In a Midwestern culture of passive communication and buried revelations, piercing communication was shocking, unsettling, and occasionally even prophetic.

Pleasantries will not save us. Nice words can't bring us home. Glad-handing is a lovely social lubricant but ineffectual for any sort of transformation. If we care more about what things look like than what they are and more about what others think of us than who we actually become, we've missed the boat entirely. Who was it that said truth was like a sword? Oh yes. Jesus.

"If we really believe all this is true," I asked my friend Clint one year at our annual evangelical family camp, "why aren't we over there telling people about it?"

I gestured across the channel to the stretch of beach where people were allowed to wear two-piece bathing suits. For all we knew, they were going to hell, without even a handbasket in sight, and someone needed to do something about it. All week we'd heard missionaries and preachers extol the importance of spreading the gospel. This was our chance.

There might have been people who believed exactly what I believed over at that neighboring beach; there were likely folks farther along their journey with Jesus than I was at the tender age of sixteen. But I had been taught to assume I knew things they did not and had a responsibility to let them know how wrong they were. And you know what they say about assuming.

"I'm not going over there," he said. Then he gestured to his sand-sprinkled towel. "I'm on vacation."

This seemed as good a reason as any.

Crows illustrate how quickly and easily we ascribe nefarious motives to what we don't understand. Smart, tricky birds? Must be evil. As a child I was suspicious of anyone who didn't attend our particular church. Clearly the Lutherans and UCC folks and Catholics were off base, because they weren't *us*. Even our two sister churches, one to the north, one to the west, were doubtful— after all, their people weren't *our* people. While children tend to begin their understanding in binaries—is that a good guy or a bad guy?—we mustn't remain there. Gospel truth is built from love, forged in love, built upon love—and love is nuanced. It has the power to see.

Yet the darkness of suspicion and the shadows of arrogance bridge the gap between the human and avian worlds. Poe's raven lives in all of us. A flock of corvids is rarely a welcome guest.

"They just make me nervous," a friend told me. "They're creepy garbage birds."

Perhaps crows are not an omen but a mirror. Garbage in, garbage out. It is out of the overflow of the heart that the mouth speaks. The nightfall we fear already lies within us.

Part of grieving my grandfather is making peace with the ways I disappointed him. He never said as much, but I know our visits were more rare than he would have liked. Young grandchildren change from day to day. How achingly much more do they transform over the span of years? Covid shut down our travel for a long time, and in the end he only met Felicity once.

Still, there's a strange beauty in naming the truth that some of my actions have been a disappointment.

Years back a therapist had me read *The Drama of the Gifted Child*, helping me untangle all the ways my desires to please everyone and control the world's feelings about me—only good! all the time! —had tied knots in my soul. Once I began to invite God into those constricted places, to let go of the need to be everyone's favorite everything, I could breathe much easier. I'd been bailing out the boats of others for decades, all without donning my own life vest.

Love your neighbor as yourself, Jesus said. It was Buechner who pointed out that this means we also have to love ourselves.

I am still parsing what it means to honor my father and mother— and grandparents, too—without being submerged by expectations that aren't mine to bear. I place no blame on them for these. Oldest children tend to be pleasers; birth order is a powerful thing. I do wish I could make faster progress, though. I expected to have a good handle on this whole thing by thirty, much less forty. But then, life is long and the journey of growing up takes as long as it takes. Those albatross chicks will get bigger, but you'd better believe they're going to do it at their own pace.

And here is where I find comfort from the crows. They tend their babies, flock together, eat, play, and rest. They are fantastically adept at being who they are, part of a divine order, created for glory and pestilence and beauty and digging in the trash. They look black as night, but in good light their feathers reveal iridescence, their tails blue and green, their heads purple, their necks sheened with silver. Like most of us, they are so much more than they first appear.

Show me a crow or a raven or a jay and I'll show you a bird content to be just that. In his old age, my grandfather grew cranky and quarrelsome. He didn't apologize much. But sometimes, he did. There's a truth there, too.

Novelist Graeme Gibson traveled to Cuba and Chile and the Galapagos Islands in search of rare hawks and songbirds and albatrosses. He gathered writings and photographed art from around the world and published it in a fascinating and beautiful collection titled *The Bedside Book of Birds*. In the last year of his life, suffering from vascular dementia, his travels were over, but his partner Margaret Atwood saw to it that he had a comfortable chair at a window overlooking their backyard bird feeder. Though the birds there were nothing noteworthy, just finches and sparrows and grackles, Graeme continued to take delight in them, once commenting, "I no longer know their names. But then, they don't know my name, either."[8]

And here it is: the truth, the core, the beating heart of it all: the earth is the Lord's and everything in it. We, too, are the creatures of God's hand. Apart from his knowledge and care, not one of us will fall. Here is our hope. Rooted, established, nurtured, grown. Here is our freedom to delight in albatrosses and sparrows, hawks and grackles, poverty and riches. Here is our patience with enemies, love for neighbors, and salvation at the end of the world.

It is in and through and with Christ. Hidden in him, the one upon whom a dove alighted. Baptized, crucified, resurrected, and ascended in glory.

There is, indeed, a deeper magic at work.

The birds know it well.

14

REST

QUAIL

Even the darkest night will end,
and the sun will rise.

VICTOR HUGO

GRANDPA'S ALUMINUM FISHING BOAT BOBS in the lapping waves. He and Grandma and my mother scan the reeds at the side of the lake for the beaver he spotted earlier. The sun beats down hard for early June in Wisconsin; I can feel my cheeks beginning to burn. My yellow Snoopy life jacket chafes under my chin.

"Can we go back now?" I ask, lying down on one of three plank seats, shielding my eyes from the glare. "Caitlyn and I were going to play ponies."

"In a minute," my mom says.

Grandpa pulls the cord to start the outboard motor again, holding down the throttle, and we begin puttering along the shoreline. I raise my head, my hair sticky with sweat, and look back toward the house. We are heading away. I sigh. I wish now that I'd stayed back with Caitlyn and Dad, though at the moment the decision was posed, going for a boat ride without my two-year-old sister seemed too good to pass up.

I run my hand along the upper ridge of the boat's side, the gunwale, feeling dots of water jump up from the spray to freckle my fingers. Then my hand encounters a bump in its path. I look up—it is the top of the hole for the oar pegs. These pegs would connect oars to the boat if need be, a safeguard in case the motor were to sputter out. I look down. Two wooden oars nestle beneath me, tucked under our plank seats. I trace the hole with my finger.

"I'm hungry," I say.

"We'll have a snack when we get back," Grandma says, lifting binoculars to her eyes. A red-winged blackbird burbles at us from the cattails. I lean back on the seat and tap my feet rhythmically against the boat's side.

"Stop it," says Grandpa.

I sigh again. My hand resumes its path until I can't reach any farther, so then I reverse its journey, tracing the gunwale back again, stopping once more at the peg hole. I wonder if my finger will fit all the way inside its three-inch tunnel. I tip my finger up and into the hole, pushing it down over an inch until my largest knuckle puts a stop to my finger's journey. My arm becomes the oar, anchored to the boat, taking us home. After a moment, the awkward angle brings an ache, so I go to pull my finger out, but— my heart drops—it won't come.

I tug quietly for a moment, panic swelling in my chest. I shift my posture to shield my plight from the adults. No one has noticed yet. I pull harder.

Quail look too good to be true. Just who do they think they are, anyway, with their forehead plumes and their smooth, plump bodies? They look like pears in black tie, like bedazzled, feathered gourds. From their gentle calls—the California Quail offers a sunny *Chi-ca-go!*—to their military formations to their love of dust baths, it doesn't take much imagination to see why Walt Disney put them in *Bambi*. I'm not one to squeal, but I can't help it with quail. They summon squealing.

The California Quail—our state bird since 1932—favors desert chaparral but will settle for backyards and parks if there's shrubbery available for nesting and cover. Like prairie dogs, quail set a watch. Males often stand as sentries atop fence posts or low branches, ready to alert the flock that it's time to explode away in a rush of beating wings and feathers, a process known as "flushing." Though they can fly, quail much prefer the ground, and the combination of their long legs and camouflage feathers allows for quick, fast sprints that end with them blending seamlessly into the landscape.

Quail are communal birds. It is rare to see one at a time and much more common to see a line of them skittering across a trail or a backyard, one after the other, a train of urgent waddling. After a male-female pair hatches their brood—usually around a dozen, but sometimes as many as twenty-eight nestlings—they often mix with other clutches, all the adults chipping in to care for the young. Notes the Cornell Lab of Ornithology, "Adults that raise young this way tend to live longer than adults that do not."[1] And there it is— the age-old truth. We can't go it alone. Or perhaps we can, but we won't do nearly as well.

The rhythms of work and rest, play and learning, celebration and grief, are intended to be lived out together in community. Together we heal. Together we grow. Together we learn.

We are all part of the flock.

Daryl and I are midsabbatical now, a few weeks into the twelve we've been given for rest and renewal, time set apart for God to work on our weary souls. I have spent these first weeks attending to my grief, turning it over and over in my hands like a beautiful stone.

I am grieving the loss of my grandfather, but the stone I hold has many other facets, too. There is the weight of pastoring through a pandemic: the burdens of leadership, the exhaustion of pivoting and pivoting and pivoting until I was so damn tired I literally thought I had a brain tumor. I grieve the apocalyptic unveiling of the church in America, who we thought we were and who we've been revealed to be.

I grieve the shattering discoveries I've made about birds while researching this book: the story of the last Kauai O'o bird, captured on film calling out for a mate who would never come. The decimated honeycreepers, the extinct Laughing Owl and Least Vermilion Flycatcher and Pagan Reed Warbler. The Ivory-billed Woodpecker no one has documented since World War II that a couple of birders in Louisiana search for day after day in a quixotic quest.[2] I grieve that 48 percent of the world's eleven thousand avian species are currently in decline, the majority due to habitat destruction, pollution, or both.[3]

I am surprised to discover that I am also grieving the end of my youth. The phrase *over the hill* might be a cliché, but something about it rings true. I can see the past four decades lined up behind me and the gentle but inevitable downward slope of what lies ahead. Rarely a day goes by when I don't think about my own mortality.

So here I am, heavy with grief but expectant in hope, too. Every day I feel the shroud over my heart lift a little more. We don't grant much time for the heavy work of big griefs, much less smaller ones.

We are a people who *overcome* and *transcend* and *just keep swimming.* But what is unexhumed remains ungrieved, and what we don't grieve will weigh us down like plastic in the belly of an albatross, accumulating over time until we risk plunging into the sea.

Each morning I wake stunned with gratitude at being given the space to do this work—work that takes the time it takes. Grief cannot be rushed. The first weeks, I hike and hike and hike. I see a trauma therapist who speaks words of kind wisdom over me as I soak her couch with tears. I do thirty jigsaw puzzles. I read Buechner and young adult novels and my friend Aarik's column about music and faith. I pick up the children from school, look into their earnest faces, and listen to the stories of their days without ever once glancing at my watch. I watch for birds. I visit friends. Slowly, the rest and respite of extended sabbath are doing their work on my soul. I am beginning, once again, to look up.

Sabbatical dovetails with the start of the fall migration, the return of the warblers and the White-crowned Sparrows. Some dear soul at church tucks a note into my mailbox with an Orange County Regional Parks Pass and a list of the sixteen forested playgrounds to which it grants access. I decide to visit them all.

It is on one of these trails that I meet my first quail.

In Exodus 16 the Israelites march through the dusty desert. They've left their enslavement behind, Pharoah and his armies an increasingly distant memory. Even the miracle of the Red Sea begins to fade in their minds as they face a pressing predicament: there is no food.

Their need is not a surprise to God; our needs never are. Yet instead of bringing their worries and requests to him, they do what comes much more naturally to most of us. They kvetch.

"If only we had died in Egypt!" they say.

Moses takes their petitions to the Lord, who responds not with a stern word—*seriously, folks, do you not remember the brick-making?*—but with divine provision. In the morning, there will be manna. In the evening, quail. Five days every week they are to gather what they need; on the sixth day, they are to gather extra, so they can rest from their labors on the sabbath. For the next forty years there is manna. For forty years, quail.

But this is just half of the story. We find the second version in Numbers 11, and, in contrast to the blessing of God in Exodus, this is not an easy tale. We don't use Numbers 11 for children's Sunday school, because *yikes*. Here's the abridged version: Moses is leading the Israelites through the desert on their way to the Promised Land. God saved them from slavery in Egypt, led them safely through the Red Sea, and is providing daily manna from heaven, yet the people are still grumpy. They might have freedom in the desert, but in Egypt they had *cucumbers*.

So they grumble against the Lord, sick of the manna, blind to the miracle, and Moses is over it. "I cannot carry all these people by myself," he tells God. "The burden is too heavy for me." Moses tells God he wishes God would just end his life rather than forcing him to face their gripes. (Truly, there isn't much that disheartens a leader more than chronic whining.) God tells Moses they will receive enough meat to satisfy them—all six hundred thousand men, plus women and children. That they will have so much meat they will get sick of it. It will be so much it will *come out of their nostrils*. Moses experiences a moment of doubt—all the flocks and herds he can imagine wouldn't be enough to feed this crowd, and there's not a goat in sight—but then he repeats to the people what God has said: *Here come the quail.*

There are so many quail that the ground is completely covered, to a depth of *three feet*. There are so many quail, the ground is covered for an *entire day's journey*. There are so many quail that each person gathers literally *over a metric ton*.[4] Thousands upon thousands of pounds of protein.

It's hard to read this story as anything but cruel hyperbole. "You want rain?" God seems to say. "Enjoy drowning!" It concludes with the complainers not sated but annihilated—struck down by a plague as the anger of the Lord burns hot against them. The survivors name the place Kibroth Hattaava—*graves of craving*. When the quail showed up in Exodus, they were straightforward provision and blessing. Here they are divine punishment, a cosmic "be careful what you ask for."

It's a fascinating story—miracle and punishment both—and it brings up scientific questions as well. Common Quail, the type found in the Sinai Peninsula, typically consume hemlock seeds during migration, making their meat toxic to humans. Was the plague mentioned in Numbers the result of this type of toxicological syndrome? It's certainly possible. A quail migration would also explain why the Israelites had no quail the day before and then, quite suddenly, an abundance. God often works within the natural laws of creation, even when performing the seemingly miraculous. (Malcolm Gladwell has a fascinating related hypothesis about the story of David and Goliath.[5])

Graves of craving. These yawning abysses lie within our own souls, too. We demand what God does not wish to give us: ease, simplicity, answers. We want to twist God's metaphorical arm until we get our way. But as Madeleine L'Engle put it, "Satan will bargain with us. God . . . will not."[6]

During my chaplaincy training I spent long days in the ICU watching people die. One day, months in, I snapped. I stomped into my supervisor's office and demanded answers.

"What do you need, Courtney?" Eileen asked, a bite of salad halfway to her mouth.

I stepped back on my heel. This was an unexpected question. What *did* I need?

"I need people to stop *dying*," I shouted. "I need an end to all this suffering. I need a better world. I need God to do his *job*."

She listened and nodded and then said, "Perhaps you might visit the maternity floor for a little while and look at the babies. Not the NICU. Go to the window in the maternity ward and look at all those fat, healthy babies."

This was insulting. The world was burning, and she was prescribing cuteness. On top of that, I am not a baby person. Give me a college student any day of the week. Or a bird. I sputtered.

"Give it a try," she said gently. "Then come back and we'll talk some more."

I wanted everything put right that very second, but Eileen, with her decades of experience around death and grief, knew there were no easy answers. She also knew that no one can flourish by looking only at suffering day in and day out. My craving for a better, more just world was not set right at the picture window in front of bassinets, but her advice was sound. After a little while my heart settled in my chest and the shadow of death withdrew as I rested on a bench and took some deep breaths and watched those babies.

Look, said a still, small voice. *Hope.*

My grandfather was not an easy person; he did not live an easy life. He was rough the way I imagine the Old Testament prophets must have been. No one was inviting Amos for tea. Elisha sent a great general on a seemingly foolish quest. Jeremiah upset people with his ranting and his foreshadowing and his obsession with ceramics. Yet the longer I live, the more the few words my grandfather did speak hold a unique presage.

My grandfather embodied a truthful wildness that the church often shies away from. Pastors—and I'm as guilty of this as any—sanitize. We brighten the grungy, tarnished events of life, repackaging messy stories for quick, pithy sermon illustrations.

"Oh, I see," the adult daughter of a pastor friend once told him. "You describe the kind of children you *wish* you had."

We try to make the best of things when God would have us, instead, speak of what truly is, even when it unsettles or challenges or takes longer than the sermon clock allows. The gospel isn't all heavenward fairy tales or circumstances that tie up neatly in a bow. The good news of Jesus is sturdy and gritty because that is what life is, and that's what life requires. Grandpa knew that, somehow. Perhaps not the Jesus part, but the reality of life, that it required perceptive, incisive truth. His responses could be weirdly profound. For one thing, death *is* bullshit.

I think about him a lot on my hikes, watching quail flush from the bushes. Like the quail, I am mostly tethered here to the ground. Someday I will fly, but for now I am down here in the dust, firmly situated upon the soil, slowly learning to look up. After the night comes the dawn. After the death will come the resurrection. After the monitor flatlines in the ICU, it is good to go visit the babies.

Above my writing desk sits a wooden cross with a rectangle of silver embedded in its center. Grandpa never had much money, but he was faithful and diligent with what he did have. After his funeral, my mother passed out bundles to my sisters and cousins and me, each wrapped in one of Grandpa's signature bandannas. We opened them together, revealing differently shaped wooden plaques, each surrounding a small silver bar. The precious metal was an investment—Grandpa was sketchy about banks—and my grandmother chose to pass them down to us. Mine is embossed with Easter lilies, a puzzling choice for one as uncomfortable with religion as he was. We held them up around the dinner circle on my parents' deck.

"It's fitting that the pastor ended up with the cross," said my mom.

"I love it," I said, and I did. I do.

In the months after the funeral, Daryl and I share memories. He points out that Grandpa's death did not solve everything that's become complicated within the family, but it didn't create any more wounds, either. This is laudable in its own right. Somehow, in his death, Grandpa became a conduit of rest within the family. Despite being a difficult person, he brought a measure of unity. I think of Saint Francis's prayer: *Lord, make me an instrument of thy peace.* The patron saint of animals surely knew something about the patience and quietness required in loving wild things. My family's honoring of my grandfather—and of one another, through gentleness and food and conversation and space, everyone bringing something to share, something to say—provided a haven.

I am learning that death is its own kind of respite. My grandfather now rests eternally from his pain and his past. The family rests in our memories of him and in our care for one another.

Looking back on our family circled up on the muggy July deck the day of his memorial, my grandmother in the seat of honor, kids bobbing and weaving underfoot, food coming in and out, I see a regal family of quail.

It is all too much to bear alone. So we do it together. Which is how it is created to be.

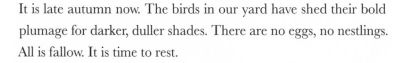

It is late autumn now. The birds in our yard have shed their bold plumage for darker, duller shades. There are no eggs, no nestlings. All is fallow. It is time to rest.

I have been afraid of taking this sabbatical because I knew my grief would rise to fill the silences. I've been running from my own heartache for so long, fearful of what it might do to me, and more afraid still of the yawning abysses of others. Grief is the tenderest possible thing. No wonder we bury it deep.

But here I am, midway through the weeks of respite, finally crying all the tears I bottled up and waking to promises I once believed that seem, somehow, like they may again hold true. I invite friends on a hike in the gloaming, the invitation itself a sign of healing for a frayed introvert, since I usually can only bear to hike alone. The trees are afire with evening light, and a dozen quail flush from the bushes in the near distance, flapping up into a cloud of *Chi-ca-go*s! We watch them go and make gentle conversation and I feel a tiny tendril of hope pushing its way up through the soil of my heart.

I remember the first moment I felt Lincoln, our oldest son, kick in my womb. *Quickening*, it is called. I was sitting on the chancel at a Lutheran church in southern Wisconsin for the town's ecumenical Good Friday service, when somewhere between the readings by the Reformed pastor and the Methodist, a gentle flutter inside my belly drew my attention from the liturgy. On the day of remembrance of Jesus' death, a sign of new life. Small, almost imperceptible, but with a promise to grow. To strengthen. To become inevitable.

The world is pregnant with hope. The birds sing of it. Press your hand to your heart. Press your feet into the ground beneath you. Can you feel the pulse of it?

My grandfather is buried in Harshaw and my family is grieving in Wisconsin and Illinois and Minnesota and here in California, and somehow the final thread of an eighty-nine-year-old man's tangled life has bound us together with a quickening of hope.

There it is: a testament and witness to the God who holds all things together.

When the adults in the boat realize my finger is stuck in the oar hole, general exasperation ensues.

"Oh Courtney," my mom says, attempting to help me wiggle my finger free before realizing it is futile. Grandpa silently turns the boat around, heading back to the house. Grandma leans over.

"I hope there's not a big spider in that hole," she says. I begin to cry.

We turn into the bay with our pier and Grandpa pulls the boat up, slings a line around a metal cleat to secure it, and heads up to the house.

"I'll be right back," he says. "I know what to try."

I sit in the hot sun, my finger swelling, tears swimming down my face. I watch the birch leaves overhead, stilled with no breeze to ruffle them, the sun's rays illuminating them to near neon. I don't know what Grandpa is going to do. I picture him at his tool bench looking for a metal saw. Is he going to cut my finger out from its metal prison? Would he cut my finger *off*? I am at his mercy, trapped here until he finds a way to free me. I can see the headline: *Girl Spends Childhood in Fishing Boat. Kindergarten Graduation Ceremony Held at Lake.* I don't want a snack anymore. I just want freedom.

I hear a footstep on the pier. I look for a glint of metal but all Grandpa holds is a plastic bottle of oil from the kitchen. He puts a hand on my arm.

"Here we go," he says, unscrewing the blue cap and tipping the oil onto my finger. "Wiggle it around, if you can, to get some oil into the hole." I wiggle. I tug. Out it pops.

I step to the pier, ready to run for the house, but something stops me. I turn.

"Thank you, Grandpa," I say.

"You know, Court," he says, taking a bandanna out of his back pocket to mop up the excess oil, "someone as smart as you are should not go sticking her finger into oar holes."

I nod. "I'm sorry," I say.

"That's okay," he says. "You're okay now."

I uncover my grief bit by bit, letting in oxygen and sunlight and the Holy Spirit. My voice begins to return to fuller strength. I walk the San Joaquin Marsh and see a half dozen types of warblers. In September, an American Oystercatcher is passing through. In October, the White-crowned Sparrows come back. Late one morning in November, I turn the corner and a Roadrunner is sitting atop a Tree Swallow's nesting box, its eyes beady, its chocolate-colored mohawk askew.

"Beep, beep," I whisper. I am beginning to see a way through.

My grandfather will always be with me. So will the ache of this loss. To be a person is to grieve.

But I've been thinking a lot about that day in Grandpa's fishing boat, the burning shame, the fear, the knowledge that I had disappointed everyone again. I remember waiting helplessly. I hear Grandpa's heavy brown shoes walking down the pier. I see the shiny bottle of canola oil in his hands. I feel his anointing, his blessing setting me free.

The Catholic church offers a liturgy of prayer for the time of death, but I've amended it as my own at the end of every day, gratitude and request.

O Lord, thank you for supporting us all the day long.
The shadows have lengthened and the evening has come.
The busy world is hushed, and the fever of life is over for today.
For now, our work is done.
Now, Lord, in thy mercy,
grant us a safe lodging,
a holy rest,
and peace at last.

15

———

HOPE

BIRDS

———

"Hope" is the thing with feathers –
That perches in the soul –
And sings the tune without the words –
And never stops – at all –

EMILY DICKINSON

HOLY WEEK BEGINS TOMORROW. My grandfather has been dead for nearly a year. Not passed away or expired. Dead. The family decides together across the miles that we will toast him on the anniversary of his death—gin, for those who can stomach it; anything else for the rest of us.

Spring has triggered fresh grief. The same jasmine plant blooms beside our front wall, its scent bringing me back to the day I wheeled a suitcase out our front door, headed to the airport to see how he was doing and, though I didn't know it, to say my final goodbye. Our bodies, attuned as they are to nature's cues—the angle of the sun, the return of the warblers, the nectarine tree spreading out its pink blossoms—remember the pain of what happened in the past around the same weeks and months. In a season of new life, I find myself preoccupied with death.

I prepare for Good Friday, trading emails with our worship director. Near the end of the service, we will recite a suspended Apostles Creed, ending with the repetition of the single line that speaks of the death of Jesus: *he was crucified, dead, and buried . . . he was crucified, dead, and buried . . . he was crucified, dead, and buried.* Then we will walk out into the night in darkness and silence.

Holy Week always feels heavy, its darkness weighing down my soul, the evil that haunts these days thick in the air like cigarette smoke. *One of you will betray me,* Jesus tells his disciples, passing bread and wine around the Passover table. We nod. *Yes, we did. Yes, we have. Yes, we will again.*

On this first anniversary, remembering my grandfather's final, painful days adds a new layer to the heaviness of Holy Week. I prepare a box of kid art and Easter chocolates to send to my grandmother. She and I text a little, but I don't call. I tell myself I'm too busy, but really, I'm afraid of adding her pain to my own. Grief can turn us inward, and I can't tell whether its selfishness or survival. Maybe it's both.

At dinner on Palm Sunday, the kids are tucking into their food at our kitchen table while Daryl's and mine grow cold. We're pingponging dozens of details—logistics, schedules, service times—across to one another, back and forth, when he stops midphrase and gasps.

"Oh wow." He rises and moves to the sliding glass door. The kids glance up.

"Mommy!" Felicity exclaims, and we walk together to the scene.

A Cooper's Hawk sits on the grass three feet from the children's backyard playhouse, its short, curved beak shining with blood.

Gripped in its talons are the remnants of a mockingbird, the breast ripped open, the black and gray and white feathers blown out in every direction as if by an explosion.

The five of us stand motionless at the window, awestruck by beauty and horror. The male hawk has muscular shoulders and stormy gray wings; its breast is speckled reddish brown and white. Its feet are powerful, gnarled, bright yellow, and its black pupils float in red-orange orbs.

"I am sad for it, Mommy," Felicity whimpers, hugging my leg as the hawk rips a strip of flesh from the carcass. The mockingbird was on the peak of our neighbor's roof this morning, singing us into spring before sunup. Lying in bed in the moment between the quiet of sleep and the shock of full awareness, before the crush of all that needed to be done at church began to crowd my mind, and before the grief came back, I had listened to it and smiled.

Watching the hawk at work, Wilson whispers, "This is *so cool*."

"It's eating dinner just like we are!" Lincoln says.

The kids go back to their food and eventually Daryl does, too, leaving me with my fingertips pressed to the cool glass. The hawk is meticulous in his work, unhurried, watchful. When nothing remains of the mockingbird but bones and feathers, the hawk lifts off and is gone.

At dusk on Holy Monday, I go down to look for warblers at the creek. It's been a wet spring and the wild mustard plants have grown eight feet high. I walk through a green and yellow forest ringing with the song of Common Yellowthroats: *Wichita Wichita Wichita*. These birds reside here year-round, but in spring they put on a real show. As I draw near the creek, Yellow Warblers join their chorus, their songs flashier than their common cousins'. I can hear them but they're tricky to spot, preferring the topmost branches, flitting about with jerky, rapid motions through the newly born leaves. I scan the highest treetops with my binoculars until my neck begins to ache. No Yellow Warblers, but suddenly a flash of red and a comical call, and I am drawn back up the trail and into a grove of oaks studded with a dozen Acorn Woodpeckers. I smile. Much of the magic of birding lies in searching for one thing and discovering another. Keep looking up, I've learned. There's almost always someone there.

Back in college, I tipped a kayak over in a dangerous stretch of rapids. I was the lead guide for a group of high school campers, they in big sturdy rubber rafts while my fellow guides and I piloted lighter, more maneuverable sit-atop kayaks. It had rained heavily, and I was particularly worried about a section of the river where the increase in flow had turned a normally easy feature into a re-circulating hole—whitewater jargon for a spot where water gets cycled back upstream, potentially trapping boats or people. In a boat, a hole can be an annoyance, usually taking strong paddling to get free. But if anyone fell out, the hole could potentially trap them under the water for far longer than a held breath.

I'd petitioned the camp's leadership to postpone the trip—with so much recent rainfall, going now seemed riskier than necessary—but they were unmoved. So I pulled extra lifeguards from the camp's beach to stand on the rocks above the troublesome section of river. They would hold throw bags—coiled ropes inside bright orange canvas—to help rescue anyone who got themselves into a bind. It wasn't much in the way of protection—they were beach guards, after all, and untrained in whitewater rescue—but it was something.

The day of the trip dawned, bluebird-bright and hot for a Wisconsin summer. Once we launched out onto the river, the teens rejoiced, showboating and splashing each other with their paddles, laughing and bouncing up and down in their rafts. All went beautifully on the easy upper sections.

By the time we reached the worrisome stretch, the lifeguards were at their posts atop the high rocks, each with a throw bag in hand, alert and ready. I held my breath as boat after boat made it across the hole, the high schoolers hollering, the guides triumphant. Finally, the last raft jostled across, and I breathed a prayer of thanks and relief as the campers sailed around the bend. The threat was behind them. I could now pull up the rear.

I pushed off with my paddle from the upstream eddy I'd been occupying and glanced up at the rocks above me, but—and here I did a double-take—they were suddenly empty of lifeguards. There was nothing over my head but a stand of trees and an expanse of blue sky. As the rapids rushed me swiftly downstream, I craned my neck—surely they hadn't left before I made it through?—and my center of gravity shifted. My kayak caught the whitewater at the lip of the hole and, in horrifying slow motion, I tumbled out of my boat and into the churning blackness.

Few natural forces hold the power that water does. Just one square meter weighs over two thousand pounds.[1] Add the speed of a river's current to that weight, and whitewater becomes much too powerful to fight against and win. As the water closed over my head, green and then frothy white and then green again, I caught alternating glimpses of the river bottom and then the sun. I struggled frantically, knowing I couldn't swim against the recirculating current but hoping perhaps an arm or leg could reach outside the hole and into the water beyond it, thereby using the river's own motion to propel me out and up. My heart screamed, but my voice remained unheard. Drowning is silent, after all. From within the river's belly, the pounding whitewater felt blank, its force utterly unconcerned with whether I lived or died.

My lungs began to burn. I was running out of time and the river refused to release me. There was only one thing left to try, a move of absolute last resort. I would remove my life vest and try to swim farther down in hopes of finding a way out from there. As I summoned all my strength to reach against the pounding water for the buckle on my vest, my elbow snagged the outside current, pulling me into the main flow of the river. Just like that, the hole gave me up. I popped into the light, gasping, too stunned to sob or scream or even speak. I lay on my back, sailing swiftly with my feet pointed downstream, blinking up at the sun.

A hundred yards further and I found my paddle caught in the reeds. Around the bend, I discovered my boat hung up between two rocks. I swam to it and took a long, shuddering breath. There was nothing to do but climb back in and finish the trip.

After loading the high schoolers onto their bus, one of the other guides put a hand on my shoulder.

"What happened?" she asked, pulling me in for a hug. "We got worried when it took you so long to meet up with us."

She leaned away to look at my face as I struggled for words. Then she gasped. "Oh no," she said, "was it the hole?" It was then that the dam of tears released.

"There was no one there," I sobbed. "I was all alone."

Over the years, as the terror faded with therapy and time, I could start to see that this wasn't the complete story. Aloneness never is. The story—our story—is one of presence. Though the lifeguards abandoned their posts one boater too soon—and believe me, they felt *terrible* when they learned of my near-calamity—there was still someone there.

When you walk through the waters, God speaks through the prophet Isaiah, *I will be with you. Do not be afraid.*

I go birding in part because it constantly makes me feel the opposite of what I felt that day on the river. When I look up, I know someone is there. A warbler, maybe, or a woodpecker. A hawk. A dove. A sparrow. I watch the birds and God watches me and I remember that we are seen and loved and held and never abandoned.

God has a long, biblical history of *sending* in order to catch our attention—first prophets, then Jesus, the Spirit, each of us. Birds are God's emissaries, too, go-betweens reminding us that to pay attention is to learn how to receive the blessings of God. They are a living meeting place of knowing God and being known by God.

Fernando Ortega once told me about trying to write a eulogy for his mentor, a man who died at the very start of the pandemic. With travel shut down, Fernando would deliver his message over Zoom. Alone at his kitchen table late at night, he searched for the right words. What could he possibly say to sum up the life and faith of a man who'd meant so much to him? How could words possibly stand in for hugs and a shared meal and human presence? We were all so horribly separated in those first days. It brings back an ache whenever I think of it.

"I got pretty weepy," he said. "It was a big loss when he passed."

Fernando had accidentally left an outside light on, and as he glanced up from his notes, he noticed a bird.

"I looked out this window and there was a little Western Screech Owl perched on a branch. They're tiny little things . . . but I felt like . . . when I saw that screechy, he was saying it was going to be okay," he said.

I asked if he felt seen by God.

"It was like that."[2]

God offers no promise of ease and few explanations this side of eternity. What we do receive is presence. And therein lies the promise—not of certainty or ease or simplicity or overcoming but of the God who was and is and will be God-with-us. We are part of a story with an arc that bends, as the Reverend King once put it, toward justice. Jesus sits with us in our sufferings and points toward a deeper, unfathomable hope.

On Sunday, Daryl gives the children's talk, with all the littles in their Easter finest crowded around the steps at the front of the chancel. He tells the story of the Cooper's Hawk and the mockingbird, of Felicity's response, and then of the heart of the gospel.

"We are called to love God and our neighbors and work for good in the world," he says, "but there are some things only God can do. I wanted to bring that mockingbird back to life. Felicity was so sad. Death is the enemy. But bringing life out of death is something only God can do. And in Jesus, death is swallowed up in victory." The children nod, some with lips and fingertips still sugared from the morning's treats.

In seminary, a few of our friends would bake a layer cake each Easter with a single word written in yellow frosting: YES. In the face of injustice and oppression, violence and evil, sin and death, the bad things we have done and the good things we have failed to do, the gulf between divine love and our feeble attempts at the same, God steps in and says, *yes. Yes, I am making all things new. Yes, there is a new kingdom at hand. Yes, there is hope beyond what we can see. Yes, there is better yet to come.*

Yes, I love you.

Yes, I am here.

Yes.

A year ago, an eighty-nine-year-old man breathed his last. There were no friends at his bedside, for the few he'd had preceded him in death. But we were there. My grandmother. My mother and father, my aunt and uncle. My sisters and cousins and me. The Holy Spirit was there, breathing the breath of hope. Each of us bore witness to a life etched with pain and strangely beautiful.

Creation sings and groans, both together.

God is present.

Look up.

ACKNOWLEDGMENTS

FIRST, THANK YOU, READER, for joining me on this journey. I wish you many warblers.

I am indebted to so many in the writing of this book. To my agent, Bob Hostetler, for being steady and wise, and to all the good folks at the Steve Laube Agency.

To Ethan McCarthy, brilliant editor and kind human, for helping this book soar (you were so very right about the final chapter!). To Cindy Bunch, Lori Neff, Terumi Echols, and the entire team over at InterVarsity Press, including David Fassett, whose cover art took my breath away. Thanks to Kristi Fender for copyediting, and Amanda Keesee and Tianna Haas for endorsement magic.

To Dale Gentry for catching my birding errata with expertise and kindness.

To Paul Wallace and his "birds from the Lord," and for sharing this phrase so generously with me and my readers.

To my birding friends—Kay, Lori, Susie, Amy, Aaric, Paul, David, Dave, Fernando, Keith, Christy, Molly, Annette, Jessica, Heather, Lauren, Frank, Nate, Bob, Traci, Tim, Joan, the other Paul, Margaret, Jodhan, Karl, Rebecca, Sean, Bekah, Elaine, Kyle, Caryn, Jocelyn, Patsy, Jenna, Becca, Janet, Tiffany, Quinn, Peyten, Eugenio, and Michelle. Thank you for teaching me about birds and helping me find hope. And to Cori George, Susan Baller-Shephard, and Leah Dean Thomas for coming up with the hilarious birdy endorsements that grace this book.

To JD Flannel Donuts in San Juan Capistrano, for the world's best sugar rush. (And gluten-free options, too! Be still, my heart!)

To Total Raptor Experience of San Diego, especially Terry and Kevin, for letting me *hold an owl*. Team Moonshine forever.

To Chris and Robbyn Upham and their children—Katherine, Gregory, Amelia, and Caroline—for the gift of Greta.

To Kassy Najm for taking me surfing.

To Beth Causey and all the gold folks at Nashville's Alive Hospice for teaching me how to gently hold vigil with those near the end of life.

To Eileen Cox, Cathy Bickerton, and Ruth Gais at Overlook Hospital for the CPE program of a lifetime.

To Nurse Beth and Doctor Freddy at Minocqua's Marshfield Hospital, for the incredibly tender care in my grandfather's final days and hours.

To Presbyterian Church of the Master and all the dear ones within our church community who have buoyed me and my family with prayers, support, love, and myriad kindnesses. Thank you for the sabbatical—my soul needed it badly and you all gave it generously. To the best church staff on the planet: Jackson, Dianne, Jeff, Kathy, Matt, Miranda, Lizzie, Kristen, Sara, Kelly, Ellie, Carol, Peter, Alyona, José, Nadine, Connor, Vanessa, Tom, and John.

To my community of friends who have walked alongside me with deep conversation, faithful prayer, and good humor: Sonia, Beth Ann and Dan (and Coert and Raymond!), Annie and Bill (and Lucy and Molly!), Ephram, Mary and Clayton, Stephanie and Chris (and Chloe and Marika!), Bethany and Joel (and Audrey, Austin, AJ, Eliza, and Henry!), Evan and Beth (and Malcolm, Thora, and

Sage!), Lilit and Stephen (and Elina and Adelie!), Vanessa and Mark, Katy and Brian (and Will, Emmie, Luke, and Olivia!), Jim and Julie (and Katie and Ellie!), Ann and Rob, Brooke and Joe, Heike, April, Harvest, Casey, Mary, Lucy and Brad (and Autumn, Delilah, and Willow!), Jonathan and Jessica (and Whit and Cor!), Inga and Jonathan, Steven and Adrian, and Mark and Kimberly.

To Kelly Rosati, who brings so many people together and who helped connect me with my new birding buddy Kay.

To the pastor friends who regularly remind me that this vocation is a wondrous calling indeed: Jon, Ross, Heather, Kathi, Tom, April, Hannah, Glenn, Steve, Jamie, David, Bill, and Roberta.

To my writing friends: Aarik, Karen, Cara, Gretchen, Holly, Heather, Laura, Collin, Michelle, Marlena, Kelsey, and Stephanie. Thank you for being companions on the journey of growing in craft. You regularly make the world—and my world—a better place.

A special word of thanks to four writer friends in particular— Alicia Akins, Steve Kamm, Bethany Rydmark, and Anna Woofenden—for their invaluable kind and honest feedback on early drafts.

To Delbert, for being the rabbit.

To my Ellis family: Tad, Sylvia, Dave and Emily (and Taylor!), Jill and Judd, Alex, Emma, Marie and Will (and Charlie!), Julie, and Deborah, for all your love and support.

To my Belcher and Snick families: Grandma Julia, whose fresh grief began just as the final edits of this book were due and we said goodbye to Grandpa Del. My parents Paul and Barb, sisters Caitlyn and Caroline, brothers-in-law Jared and Michael, nieces Aleah, Sophi, Haven, and Pippa, and nephews Hudson and Arlo, my aunt and uncle and cousins, and Grandma Ila, for living this story alongside me and for walking the steep road of grief together with such tenderness.

To my children, Lincoln, Wilson, and Felicity, for putting up with so many dinner table birding facts. You three give me so very many reasons to keep looking up.

And to Daryl, my love always and forever. You are the wind beneath my wings.

APPENDIX

SO YOU WANT TO START BIRDING?

Welcome to the wonderful world of birds! Resources abound, and I'm excited to introduce you to a few of my favorites. One of the best ways to learn more about birds is to visit a birding group—most places in the United States and Canada (and elsewhere around the world!) have one. Here you'll meet local bird aficionados who will know the best places nearby to see birds. (These hotspots may be surprisingly different from what you might expect. For example, birds love a good sewage pond!) Birders tend to be a friendly bunch, and visiting a group or joining a free hike is a great way to become initiated into the practice and have many of your questions answered.

Beyond that, here are a few tools to give you a start.

MERLIN BIRD ID

This free app from the Cornell Lab of Ornithology features easy ways to identify avian species, from visual cues (how big is it? what color? where did you see it?) to sound recordings. Since birds are more often heard than seen, the sound ID option is particularly helpful and fun. Don't forget to download the "bird pack" for your local area (mine is the Western United States) or anywhere you travel so you can take full advantage of its features.

BINOCULARS

You can go birding without these, but it's much easier (and more enjoyable) with them! Birds tend to be small, fast, and far away. Binoculars bring them close, making identification and observation much easier. For even a decent starter pair of bins, be prepared to spend over a hundred dollars. High-end pairs run in the thousands, but remember you'll likely be taking these on trails and out into the elements, so it's okay to begin with solid basics. I've been birding with a $130 pair of Nikon Prostaff 8x42s for years, and they rarely let me down.

THE NATIONAL GEOGRAPHIC GUIDE TO THE BIRDS OF NORTH AMERICA

Considered one of the gold standard field guides, this book is small enough to carry on a hike without weighing you down. Its full-color illustrations, helpful tips about distinguishing similar birds from one another, and information on where a particular bird might be spotted (and in what season!) make it a great companion for newbie birders and experts alike.

THE SIBLEY GUIDE TO BIRDS

David Allen Sibley is a legend in the birding community, both for his extensive knowledge of birds and for the invitational way he imparts that knowledge to others. There's this guide—a beautiful but hefty one, at 624 pages—as well as two shorter versions, one specifically for western birds of the United States, and one for eastern birds. If you don't travel far, investing in one of the two smaller geographical guides may be the best fit.

A LOCAL FIELD GUIDE

Purchasing a pocket-sized guide to the birds of your particular area can be a game-changer. Take it with you on your hikes or leave it by your birdwatching window. The Cornell Lab of Ornithology publishes a wonderful series and Sibley offers laminated pamphlets that you can take on even your rainiest outing.

AMERICAN BIRDING PODCAST

There are a lot of birding podcasts out there, and I can't get enough of them. But if I had to pick only one, this would be it. Host Nate Swick is knowledgeable and thoughtful, and he keeps the fun in birding. From regular rare bird alerts to ornithological marvels (truly, I never knew molting could be so fascinating!), to a brilliant assortment of guests, I regularly look forward to learning from this weekly show from the American Birding Association (ABA).

THE THING WITH FEATHERS PODCAST

Okay, shameless plug: I host this one. But hey—it's good! *TTWF* is all about birds and hope, featuring bird and birding-adjacent topics with a wide array of guests, from Christian authors, pastors, and poets who are hobby birders to expert ornithologists, ecologists, and biologists. Often there is a faith angle; other times we focus on the marvels of the birds themselves. We laugh quite a bit, too. (Plus, my two younger kids helped with the intro, and they're awfully cute.)

BIRDING MAGAZINE

This publication from the American Birding Association is a delight. It covers science, exploration, conservation, personal interest, the newest gear, and the fun of birding, too. The book review section is particularly helpful and the photos are top-notch. Once they even sent out stickers featuring the ABA's Bird of the Year. I would be lying if I told you I didn't look forward to those stickers with the enthusiasm of a kindergartener. Give me all the bird stickers.

BirdCast

This website (birdcast.info) highlights nightly bird migrations throughout the United States. I was gobsmacked to learn there are nights in the spring and fall when more than three hundred *million* birds are winging their way overhead at the same time. BirdCast is most interesting to look at during peak migratory periods (March through May and mid-August through mid-November), and you can look at an overview of the entire United States or type in your county to get nightly updates on which birds are migrating to—or through—your area. Then you can go out and search for them the next morning!

Birding scope

If you're looking to get a really good view of birds, a scope will be your new best friend. A birding scope is basically a short-range telescope: it will allow you to focus in much closer than most binoculars do. Birding scopes are pricey, so I advise people to begin with binoculars until they're sure birding is a passion that will stick. You'll want to pair it with a tripod so it's steady enough for viewing. (Also, scopes can be quite heavy, so carrying them on a hike is a real commitment. They tend to be best for birdwatching from a settled location.) The Celestron Trailseeker 65 usually retails for hundreds of dollars less than other starter scopes (under $300 as opposed to the $600 to $700 range for typical scopes of its caliber) and comes recommended by the Audubon Society.

eBird

Once you have a bit of birding under your belt, it's time for eBird. This more advanced app helps you see what species are in your area, track a life list (if you choose), and connect with other birders. Run by the Cornell Lab, eBird gathers information used by ornithologists and other scientists around the country to track migration patterns, the rise or decline of bird species, and interesting vagrants and rarities. It's citizen science at its best, and fun to boot!

NOTES

1. LOOKING UP: BIRDING

[1] Robert Service, "The Three Voices," *The Spell of the Yukon and Other Verses* (Orinda, CA: Seawolf Press, 2021), 7.

[2] See 1 Thessalonians 4:13-14.

[3] See Matthew 6:26.

[4] See Exodus 3:1-6.

[5] See Genesis 15:1-5.

[6] David Wright, "What I Wish You'd Heard," *Lines from the Provinces* (Great Unpublished, 2000), 42. Used with permission.

[7] Rowan Williams, *Being Disciples* (Grand Rapids, MI: Eerdmans, 2016), 4-5. Many thanks to Ethan McCarthy for connecting me to this beautiful book.

2. DEATH: VULTURES

[1] See Job 19:25.

[2] See John 11:25.

[3] See Revelation 1:17-18.

[4] Eugene Peterson, *Tell It Slant* (Grand Rapids, MI: Eerdmans, 2012), 70.

[5] Noah Strycker, "Spark Bird," *This American Life*, November 26, 2021, www.thisamericanlife.org/754/spark-bird.

[6] This passage is adapted from Courtney Ellis, "It Would Be Great If It Could Feature Some Clowning," *Fathom Mag*, November 18, 2018, www.fathommag.com/stories/it-would-be-great-if-it-could-feature-some-clowning. Used with permission.

3. UNCERTAINTY: MOCKINGBIRDS

[1] "How Reliable Are Weather Forecasts?" National Oceanic and Atmospheric Administration, SciJinks, https://scijinks.gov/forecast-reliability, accessed March 13, 2023.

[2] Nicolas Weiler, "A Bedtime Story," *Stanford Magazine*, September/October 2014, https://stanfordmag.org/contents/a-bedtime-story.

[3] Samuel Eliot Morison, "Harvard Seals and Arms," *The Harvard Graduates' Magazine*, September 1933, https://guides.library.harvard.edu/ld.php?content_id=44884193.

[4] Eric C. Anderson et al., "The Relationship Between Uncertainty and Affect," *Frontiers in Psychology* 10 (November 2019): www.frontiersin.org/articles/10.3389/fpsyg.2019.02504/full.

[5]Associated Press, "California Church Leaders, Shooting Survivors Join in Prayer," Voice of America, May 22, 2022, www.voanews.com/a/california-church-leaders-shooting-survivors-join-in-prayer/6584619.html.

[6]Henri Nouwen, *The Return of the Prodigal Son: A Story of Homecoming* (New York: Doubleday, 1994), 129.

[7]Samuel Beckett, "The Unnamable," in *Three Novels: Molloy, Malone Dies, The Unnamable* (New York: Grove, 1958), 387.

[8]Jennifer Ackerman, *The Genius of Birds* (New York: Penguin, 2016), 136.

[9]"Northern Mockingbird Overview," All About Birds, The Cornell Lab, copyright 2023, www.allaboutbirds.org/guide/NorthernMockingbird/overview.

[10]Linton Weeks, "Hats Off to Women Who Saved the Birds," NPR History Dept., NPR, July 15, 2015, www.npr.org/sections/npr-history-dept/2015/07/15/422860307/hats-off-to-women-who-saved-the-birds.

[11]Wendell Berry, endorsement for Charles E. Little's *The Dying of the Trees* (New York: Penguin, 1997), www.ecobooks.com/books/dying.htm.

[12]"ABA Code of Birding Ethics," American Birding Association, www.aba.org/aba-code-of-birding-ethics, accessed March 13, 2023.

[13]See Job 38.

[14]Jessica Kantrowitz (@jfkantrowitz), "You are not alone, and this will not last forever," Twitter, April 1, 2020, 8:09 p.m., https://twitter.com/jfkantrowitz/status/1565869628844277762.

[15]Ackerman, *The Genius of Birds*, 140.

[16]Oscar Wilde, *The Importance of Being Earnest* (Chicago: RR Donnelly, 1990), 14.

4. LIFE: SPARROWS

[1]Jessica Winter, "Do the Kindly Brontosaurus," *Independent*, August 17, 2013, www.independent.co.uk/news/uk/home-news/do-the-kindly-brontosaurus-the-prehistoric-pose-that-can-get-you-what-you-want-8771509.html.

[2]C. S. Lewis, *The Weight of Glory* (New York: HarperOne, 2001), 47.

[3]Mark Labberton, ed., *Still Evangelical* (Downers Grove, IL: InterVarsity Press, 2018), 30.

[4]Helen Briggs, "More Than a Billion Sparrows in the World, Study Finds," BBC News, May 18, 2021, www.bbc.com/news/science-environment-57150571.

[5]Rob Dunn, "The Story of the Most Common Bird in the World," *Smithsonian Magazine*, March 2, 2012, www.smithsonianmag.com/science-nature/the-story-of-the-most-common-bird-in-the-world-113046500.

[6]Patrick F. Houlihan, *The Natural History of Egypt*, vol. 1, *The Birds of Ancient Egypt* (Oxford, UK: Aris & Phillips, 1986), 136-37.

[7]"Red China: Death to Sparrows," *Time*, May 5, 1958, https://content.time.com/time/subscriber/article/0,33009,863327,00.html.

[8]See Matthew 10:29.

[9]See Isaiah 6:9.

[10]Dan Vahaba, "Birds Shuffle and Repeat Their Tunes to Keep Their Audience Listening," *Duke Today*, January 2022, https://today.duke.edu/2022/01/birds-shuffle-and-repeat-their-tunes-keep-audience-listening.

[11]See Psalm 96.

[12]Robin Catalano, "Could a Birding Boom in the U.S. Help Conservation Take Flight?," *National Geographic*, September 2, 2021, www.nationalgeographic.com/travel/article/could-a-boom-in-us-birding-help-fund-conservation.

[13]Gillian Flaccus, "Bird-Watching Soars Amid COVID-19 as Americans Head Outdoors," AP News, May 2, 2020, https://apnews.com/article/us-news-ap-top-news-ca-state-wire-or-state-wire-virus-outbreak-94a1ea5938943d8a70fe794e9f629b13.

5. END TIMES: OWLS

[1]Heimo Mikkola, *Owls of the World* (Chapel Hill, NC: Firefly Books, 2019), 17.

[2]Mikkola, *Owls of the World*, 18.

[3]T. S. Eliot, "The Hollow Men," *Poems: 1909–1925* (London: Faber & Faber, 1925).

[4]Makoto Fujimura, *Art and Faith* (New Haven, CT: Yale, 2020), 83.

[5]See 1 Thessalonians 5:3.

6. DAILINESS: HOUSE FINCHES

[1]Lauren Sandler, "The Secret to Being Both a Successful Writer and a Mother: Have Just One Kid," *The Atlantic*, June 2013, www.theatlantic.com/sexes/archive/2013/06/the-secret-to-being-both-a-successful-writer-and-a-mother-have-just-one-kid/276642.

[2]Jim Gaffigan, *Beyond the Pale* (New York: Comedy Central Records, 2006).

7. BROKENNESS AND SIN: HUMMINGBIRDS

[1]Aldo Leopold, *Round River* (New York: Oxford University Press, 1993), 165. Many thanks to Dale Gentry for introducing me to this quote.

[2]Sam Anderson, "The Last Two Northern White Rhinos on Earth," *New York Times*, January 6, 2021, www.nytimes.com/2021/01/06/magazine/the-last-two-northern-white-rhinos-on-earth.html.

[3]Gretchen Ronnevik (@garonnevik), "I shut my laptop. I can't deal with death today," Twitter, May 24, 2022, 5:43 p.m., https://twitter.com/garonnevik/status/1529231543633575936.

[4]Dietrich Bonhoeffer, *Life Together* (New York: Harper & Row, 1954), 91.

[5]"Rufous Hummingbird," All About Birds, The Cornell Lab, copyright 2023, www.allaboutbirds.org/guide/Rufous_Hummingbird/overview.

[6]Ed Yong, "How Animals Perceive the World," *The Atlantic*, June 13, 2022, www.theatlantic.com/magazine/archive/2022/07/light-noise-pollution-animal-sensory-impact/638446.

8. DELIGHT: WARBLERS

[1]Robert M. Pirsig, *Zen and the Art of Motorcycle Maintenance* (New York: Mariner Books, 2005), 4.

[2]Mike Bergin, "Wood Warbler Names Done Right," 10,000 Birds, June 25, 2019, www.10000birds.com/wood-warbler-names-done-right.htm.

[3]Herb Wilson, "Nocturnal Migration," *Maine Birds*, November 9, 2011, https://web .colby.edu/mainebirds/2011/11/09/nocturnal-migration.

[4]Kenn Kaufman, "Spring Migration: It's All About Timing," The National Wildlife Federation, April 7, 2010, www.nwf.org/Magazines/National-Wildlife/2010 /Migration-timing.

[5]Ross Gay, *The Book of Delights* (Chapel Hill, NC: Algonquin Books, 2022), xii.

[6]Brené Brown, *Dare to Lead* (New York: Random House, 2018), 81.

[7]William Carlos Williams, in *The Letters of Denise Levertov and William Carlos Williams*, Christopher MacGowan, ed. (New York: New Direction, 1998), 2-3.

[8]Williams, *Letters*, 4.

[9]Noah Strycker and Ira Glass, "754: Spark Bird," *This American Life*, November 26, 2021, www.thisamericanlife.org/754/spark-bird.

9. Grief: Albatrosses

[1]Ed Yong, "What a Grieving Orca Tells Us," *The Atlantic*, August, 2018, www .theatlantic.com/science/archive/2018/08/orca-family-grief/567470.

[2]Bill Chappell, "Wisdom the Albatross," NPR, March 20, 2021, www.npr.org/2021 /03/05/973992408/wisdom-the-albatross-now-70-hatches-yet-another-chick.

[3]Kennedy Warne, "The Amazing Albatrosses," *Smithsonian Magazine*, September 2007, www.smithsonianmag.com/science-nature/the-amazing-albatrosses-162515529.

[4]Michael Berger, "Till Death Do Them Part: 8 Birds that Mate for Life," Audubon Society, February 10, 2012, www.audubon.org/news/till-death-do-them-part-8-birds -mate-life.

[5]Scott Cairns, *The End of Suffering* (Brewster, MA: Paraclete, 2009), x-xi.

[6]Madeleine L'Engle, *A Stone for a Pillow* (New York: Penguin, 2017), 143.

[7]Warne, "Amazing Albatrosses."

[8]Shireen Gonzaga, "The March 2011 Tsunami Toll on Wildlife at the Midway Atoll," *Earth Sky*, March 24, 2011, https://earthsky.org/earth/the-march-2011-tsunami -toll-on-wildlife-at-the-midway-atoll.

[9]Matthew Godbey, "'Albatross' Film Explores Impact of Plastic Waste on Bird Population," *Post and Courier*, September 14, 2020, www.postandcourier.com/charleston _scene/albatross-film-explores-impact-of-plastic-waste-on-bird-population/article _e2d0002a-b04c-11e7-8ddd-6f81d2f72add.html.

[10]Nick Paton Walsh, "These Birds Are Choking on a Plastic Ocean," CNN, December 12, 2016, www.cnn.com/2016/12/11/world/vanishing-walsh-plastic-albatross /index.html.

[11]Rachel Carson, *Silent Spring* (New York: Mariner Books, 2002), 51.

10. Partnership: Wrens

[1]Aristotle, "Book IX, 1," *The History of Animals*, trans. D'Arcy Wentworth Thompson, https://penelope.uchicago.edu/aristotle/histanimals9.html, accessed June 17, 2023.

[2]Jennifer Ackerman, *The Genius of Birds* (New York: Penguin, 2016), 120.

[3]Ackerman, *Genius of Birds*, 143.

[4]Daniel A. Cox, "The State of American Friendship: Change, Challenges, and Loss," Survey Center on American Life, June 8, 2021, www.americansurveycenter.org /research/the-state-of-american-friendship-change-challenges-and-loss.

[5]Jackson Clelland, "Discovering Hope," Presbyterian Church of the Master, April 17, 2022.

11. PEACE: DOVES

[1]Peter Pap et al., "Interspecific Variation in the Structural Properties of Flight Feathers in Birds Indicates Adaptation to Flight Requirements and Habitat," *Functional Ecology* 29, no. 6 (June 2015): 746-57.

[2]"Pope's Peace Doves Attacked by Crow and Seagull," *BBC News*, January 26, 2014, www.bbc.com/news/world-europe-25905108.

[3]Justin Worland, "Balloons Replace Doves as the Vatican Symbol of Peace," *Time*, January 25, 2015, https://time.com/3681726/vatican-balloons-doves.

[4]Mary Oliver, "Maybe," *New and Selected Poems, Volume One* (Boston: Beacon Press, 1992).

[5]Jonathan Alderfer, *National Geographic's Complete Birds of North America* (Washington, DC: National Geographic, 2017), 296.

[6]This paragraph is adapted from Courtney Ellis, "A Deeper Magic," *Fathom Mag*, February 11, 2021, www.thelift.fathomcolumns.com/post/a-deeper-magic. Used with permission.

[7]Aditya Raj Kaul (@AdityaRajKaul), "A woman did her regular aerobics class . . ." Twitter, February 1, 2021, 12:55 p.m., https://twitter.com/AdityaRajKaul /status/1356315137976672259.

[8]Octavia Butler, *Parable of the Sower* (New York: Grand Central Publishing, 1993), 263.

[9]See Jeremiah 6:14.

[10]Marcia Z. Nelson, "N.T. Wright: On Jesus and Writing," *Publishers Weekly*, November 23, 2011, www.publishersweekly.com/pw/by-topic/industry-news/religion/article /49621-n-t-wright-on-jesus-and-writing.html.

[11]W. H. Auden, "For the Time Being: A Christmas Oratorio," The Poetry Hour, copyright 2023, www.thepoetryhour.com/poems/for-the-time-being-a-christmas-oratorio.

[12]Carl Sandburg, "Fog," *Chicago Poems* (New York: Henry Hold and Company, 1916).

[13]Madeleine L'Engle, *A Stone for a Pillow* (New York: Convergent, 1986), 181.

12. LOVE: PELICANS

[1]Ethel Dilouambaka, "The Story Behind Petros the Pelican, Mascot of Mykonos," *Culture Trip*, December 22, 2017, https://theculturetrip.com/europe/greece/articles /the-story-behind-petros-the-pelican-mascot-of-mykonos.

[2]"Pelican," Wikipedia, https://en.wikipedia.org/wiki/pelican, accessed June 13, 2023.

[3]Graeme Gibson, *The Bedside Book of Birds* (New York: Doubleday, 2021), xiii.

[4]"Brown Pelican: All About Birds," All About Birds, The Cornell Lab, copyright 2023, www.allaboutbirds.org/guide/Brown_Pelican/overview.

[5]Kenneth Bailey, *Jesus Through Middle Eastern Eyes* (Downers Grove, IL: InterVarsity Press, 2008), 68.

[6]Eugene Peterson, *Working the Angles* (Grand Rapids, MI: Eerdmans, 1989), 155-56.

[7]Annie Dillard, *Pilgrim at Tinker Creek* (New York: Harper, 2013), 107.

[8]This paragraph adapted from Courtney Ellis, "A Specific Love," *Fathom Mag*, March 25, 2021, www.thelift.fathomcolumns.com/post/a-specific-love. Used with permission.

13. TRUTH AND BEAUTY: CORVIDS

[1]Kyle Meyaard-Schaap, "24: Living More Gently on the Earth," June 26, 2023, in *The Thing With Feathers*, podcast, hosted by Courtney Ellis, https://open.spotify.com /show/2hV7NgvWDkNTOoRHXSQgc9.

[2]N. T. Wright, "The New Testament Doesn't Say What Most People Think It Does About Heaven," *Time*, December 16, 2019, https://time.com/5743505/new-testament-heaven.

[3]Ellen Davis, *Getting Involved with God: Rediscovering the Old Testament* (Boston: Cowley Publications, 2001), 152.

[4]Thomas Aquinas, *Summa Theologica*, q. 65, a. 1.

[5]Saint Augustine, *Sermons*, (New York: Cima Pub Co., 1947), 241.

[6]Lyanda Lynn Haupt, *Crow Planet* (New York: Back Bay Books, 2009), 69.

[7]Haupt, *Crow Planet*, 27.

[8]Gibson, *The Bedside Book of Birds* (New York: Doubleday, 2021), xv.

14. REST: QUAIL

[1]"California Quail," All About Birds, The Cornell Lab, copyright 2023, www .allaboutbirds.org/guide/California_Quail/overview.

[2]Rachel Ramirez, "Is the Ivory-Billed Woodpecker Extinct?," CNN, October 29, 2022, www.cnn.com/interactive/2022/us/ivory-billed-woodpecker-extinct-courtman -climate-ctpr.

[3]Richa Malhotra, "Habitat Loss Pushing More Birds to Near-Extinction," *Nature India*, May 18, 2022, www.nature.com/articles/d44151-022-00053-1.

[4]I'm not making this up. For reals. See Numbers 11:32.

[5]Malcolm Gladwell and Guy Raz, "What's the Real Story of David and Goliath?," TED Radio Hour, NPR, November 15, 2013, www.npr.org/transcripts/243294593.

[6]Madeleine L'Engle, *A Stone for a Pillow* (New York: Convergent, 1986), 243.

15. HOPE: BIRDS

[1]Ellie Friedmann, "The Six Most Common River Hazards," Whitewater Guidebook, May 22, 2020, www.whitewaterguidebook.com/the-six-most-common-river-hazards.

[2]Fernando Ortega, "07: The Urgency of Birding and the Power of Silence," February 27, 2023, in *The Thing With Feathers,* podcast, hosted by Courtney Ellis, https:// open.spotify.com/show/2hV7NgvWDkNTOoRHXSQgc9.